Letters on Prayer

An exchange on prayer and faith

MARK ALLEN AND RUTH BURROWS

Letters on Prayer

An exchange on prayer and faith

SHEED AND WARD
LONDON

ISBN 0–7220–4930–7

Published in Great Britain by
Sheed & Ward Limited
14 Coopers Row
London EC3N 2BH

Production and typesetting: Bill Ireson

Printed and bound in Great Britain by
Biddles Limited, Guildford and Kings Lynn

You ought always to pray and never lose heart
(LUKE 18:1)

Contents

What is prayer? Why is it so difficult to get hold of what we mean by prayer? People are asking and searching for this dimension of human life. Books on different styles of prayer seem to duck the fundamental question, 'What is prayer?' Our own experience of it is uncertain and inarticulate. It is difficult to get the confidence which helps us persevere. You have spoken of the absolute necessity for prayer, every day. What is this prayer?

Prayer is what God does in us, not what we do. Unthinkable that God is not hearing the desire to pray and seeing the effort. The simplicity of prayer. Listening to your own experience. Relationship. The Other who cares and loves us. We have to use images for a dimension which is not available to ordinary consciousness. Only in Jesus can we know the You and know the self to whom He speaks. What must I do to receive You?

Faith is the issue – faith that God is praying in us in our

prayer. Our urge towards this dimension of transcendence can appear to be from the self, rather than in reply to Another calling. Faith needed to break away from this self-absorption and to listen to God. It takes faith to 'listen' on a dimension which is 'beyond our ordinary consciousness'. Isn't our first prayer an asking for faith? You focus on Jesus. How easy it is to assent to Christianity, but to avoid this focus.

IV Seriousness about the natural ground of faith   10

There is a natural ground of Faith and it can be worked – reflected on. To begin to respond to this Someone is the beginning of Faith. False, self-orientated expectations – 'an interest in prayer'. This has little to do with the God who is. We must be serious, our surrender genuine, refuse to demand any immediate satisfaction, or pay off. Prayer is the surrender of the whole self to God. And divine Love is always seeking the human heart.

V Scripture   13

Difficulty in penetrating the familiarity of Scripture. Looking into the self: Do you mean that we can learn more of Jesus by letting him explore our own experience, rather than by our trying to reach his? Faith and Mind: to what work can we put the mind to open it to faith and prayer?

VI Faith and fidelity   15

In prayer we must stand on objective truth and not our subjective feelings. Yet we need to look into the heart, pay

attention to its experience and discover, through prayer,
who we really are, finding our true selves. Objective truth
must also be my truth, at the centre of my heart.

VII Affirming objective truth 16

Making objective truth my own: using the words of the
gospel and living from them, on them, by them. Those who
pray of two types: the naturally religious and intuitive and
those who must depend on mind alone. Faith is independent
of types and its test the same: do they pray on? Dying to the
self and the world. We surrender to a reality which cannot
be tested or proved, only affirmed through Jesus. His faith
is mine. Fidelity to prayer the clearest affirmation and, day
in day, out it has a special purity.

VIII A knowledge which is lived 19

I summarise the ground covered so far. Letting the Word
work at the self. Avoiding the trap of intellectual truth. You
speak of The Truth. How we naturally tend to evade it and
its searching power. Our lack of generosity in responding
to the Love which seeks us. 'Lived knowledge' and
intellectual apprehension. The seriousness of the problem
of faith.

IX The test of charity 23

Yes, the gulf between intellectual knowledge and real
knowledge – it can appear in talk of 'spiritual poverty'. The
test of charity may not be at the level of international

events, but at home and it is there we learn Jesus' meaning of charity: putting others before self.

Our practice of prayer may not be much changed since much earlier in life. The awkwardness of this dislocation – we don't seem able to pray where we feel we are. Early memories of petitionary prayer. The woman who found herself only asking for herself and gave up. We come close to prayer and veer off. Is petitionary prayer not a good way of holding on?

Is whether or not we pray on a par with whether we take up some interest or pastime? Desire and motive are decisive. You examine the situation of the woman faltering in prayer, her poised and uncommitted state. The need for reflection on that Presence, leading to reflection on Jesus. The imperative of seriousness. We have to make decisive choices, even at a cost to ourselves.

Christian existence itself petition. We are here to receive, 'be done unto'. The liturgy dwells on asking. Praise is difficult, but it can make sense through, in and with Jesus. Every day needs press us to petitionary prayer. Paul encourages the Church to ask. We ask from where we are and God does not despise us in our weakness. Petitionary prayer our way of staying in touch in our daily round. The faltering woman had made a start, why not persevere? We

*can help one another and need one another in this. All
prayer is answered, but how, in what way, I leave to God.*

*Some questions of method. Dangers in some 'meditational
methods'. True prayer is for all. Prayer our act of faith
which is a 'Yes' to God's desire to work in us. What we do
is not so important. Distractions a natural difficulty and
temptation. Fidelity to 'unoccupied' prayer exposes us to
God, helps us to live in Him.*

Unoccupied prayer. Prayer in the liturgy is perhaps the
experience of most and perhaps we feel safer with it. Hans
Urs von Balthazar on the prayer of the laity and the Office.
Unoccupied prayer must not be avoided – it confronts us
with the demands of faith and our real selves.

*Two aspects of Christian being: community and
solitariness. In unoccupied prayer we are undefended,
exposed to the gaze of Love. Mary and Martha. The direct
encounter of prayer creates personhood. Overcoming
self-love towards self-surrender in faith, the purest,
personal expression of prayer.*

Our resistance to progress in prayer: a fear of presumption
which is also an evasion of God's love. You insist that the
Christian response be unqualified, enduring being at the
edge, showing that we have to move from where we are.

This going to the edge a giving in or giving away. We cannot make a movement forward, only reduce resistance to it.

Our blindness in ducking the life to which we are called. Coming to recognise the nature of true prayer: recognising that God is. What blocks this recognition? Fear. We can only treat fear by turning to Jesus and his unfailing love. 'Prayer' can be our refuge from this, but prayer is also God's opportunity. The breakthrough will come at the right time, but it needs assent. So yes, letting go: a real choice and a hard paradox of experience: dying we live. We need a childlike trust in surrender. God, silent and hidden, tests our faith and we can be frightened by the absence of reassurance. Jesus asleep in the boat in the storm.

We fear release from our comforting ambiguity. Freed, we confront a reality which impels conversion. But it does not answer faith. Jesus in the boat did not answer their question, 'Who is this?' Faith is pulled further on: even what is immediate cannot be comprehended. The heart is quieter and learns in secret. Jesus in his sacrifice shows us how to endure in this faith.

Deep emotion may attend the miracle of conversion. What do we mean by 'heart'? The capacity for response to values and ideals and for conviction. Conversion may grow amid the interplay of this capacity and divine revelation. In the end, the Holy Spirit bridges the gap between belief and unbelief. Our cooperation with the Holy Spirit needs support and we have to work to get it – from books or friends. The grace of this help is all around us, but we have to use it. The effort between wishful thinking and real choice.

*and perseverance. Jesus our guide. Spiritual
poverty – knowing the pain of this purification. St
Thérèse's paradigm of the face of Jesus in his passion.
We lose our lives in order to live in Christ. Self-loss a
key to exposure which is pure prayer.*

'Unoccupied' prayer opens us to God's secret action and to a purifying experience of ourselves. We are called onwards – by a Person. LaCugna on personhood. We are called to share and share again a goodness which is God's alone. Not so much consolation, as Hope. How are these different?

We meet Christ in the Word. Trying to conform ourselves to Christ, we become open to his transforming action. St John on the Word. Unoccupied prayer affirms faith in this secret action. Coping with the weather in life and so with the weather in the soul. St Thérèse: faith, hope and love, no matter what is felt. Transformation to personhood in this life in darkness. Revelation of our divine 'sonship' is our hope, when each meets the vision of God as He is.

Images of consolations – yes we see them off, leave them be. Where we started – resolving an impasse. You have set out the fundamental principles and ideas.

The problem is lack of faith. We must work to believe to centre our thoughts on God's revelation of Himself in Jesus. There is no 'know-how'. If we believe, we trust. We don't believe when we worry. Accepting God's love of me.

*Believing precipitates prayer. Humility. Some structure
needed, but keeping relational is the key. The sacraments
are vital, the reality of His Church.*

Your salutary letter. Rahner's 'sacristy' metaphor. Being
clear between weaknesses about faith and weak faith. Weak
but real. Avoiding fretting; being of good heart. Prayer is
faith; faith is prayer.

'To know Him, love Him and serve Him . . . ' We have
ideas about knowing God and serving Him, but 'How do I
love You?' remains a hard question. In prayer, ideas of love
are so different from our human experience of it. Yet the
saints speak of 'being in love'. God's love is a mystery,
but it is given. 'Love too is what God does in us'. Jesus'
teaching on love at the Last Supper. Faith, Hope and Love:
in our prayer the Spirit mediates these gifts which we can
only understand in Jesus.

*Prayer is self-surrender in faith. Faith is self-surrender.
Faith and prayer the living relationship of love. Speaking
of this love may represent emotion and not necessarily
the reality of the relationship. God's love leads us to love,
it is given. The gospel image of the child steadies our
blindness which seeks to save ourselves. The Holy Spirit
gives us the love with which to love God. 'Unoccupied'*

prayer expresses our trust that God will do this, it is content without the joy of seeing the beauty which God sees in us, like the gull at rest on the ocean of His love.

Publisher's note

For the convenience of readers, Mark Allen's letters have been set in Roman type throughout, and Ruth Burrows's letters in italic type.

Letters on Prayer

I What is prayer?

Very dear Ruth,

Lent again. I hope you have a good Lent. You were much in mind the other day – the Cathedral here is running a series of talks on prayer for Lent and I went along to one of them. There were lots of people there, perhaps a hundred and more. We all sat on easy to stack little chairs, looking ahead like children waiting for a film to start at school.

Halfway through, the speaker startled me by asking us if we would each turn to our neighbour and ask each other what we thought prayer was. I was sitting next to a nun. Before the talk she had told me that she was retired. She looked at me now with the most marvellous smiling brown eyes, with a sort of 'Don't you dare' glint in them. I felt very self-conscious too and so just said, 'Whatever it was, why don't we each just take it home and think about it later?' She gave me a wink. Everyone else kept talking until brought to order by the speaker. The speaker went on for nearly an hour and a half. She spoke at length about God's action in our lives. But she didn't, if I may say so, deal with the core question which she made us put to each other and which, in our case, we were unable to answer out loud. What is prayer?

As the talk went on, my mind returned to a conversation you and I had nearly two summers ago. You had shown me the first half of the draft for your book *Living in Mystery* and we were talking about it. You said that the first part of the book was really getting the ground cleared for the second which you thought would be the important part: you would be dealing with the all-important subject of prayer. I told you later that I did not think that you had done so. This, as you know, was no kind of criticism of the book which I thought was dynamic and powerful, especially the later chapters. You were writing about living in mystery, about a way of life, rather, I thought, than those times in your day which you give to prayer.

Perched among the crowd in the Cathedral Hall, I thought about this soap-in-the-bath problem of prayer. Why is it so difficult to get hold of what we mean by it? There were lots of people there. So there must be a need for help about this. Are we all faltering in confidence, asking and searching for access to this dimension of human life – prayer?

'What is prayer?' That may not have been an obvious question in earlier times when people lived in a culture permeated with religion, or at least religious observance. Today, books on prayer often assume some common ground, that people really know what prayer is. There is discussion of different styles of prayer. The fundamental question, 'What is prayer?' seems to be avoided. Yet, in our own prayer, in restlessness, how do we confront it?

We are brought face-to-face with our inability to say very much about it. We are inarticulate. Inside, we may be inarticulate to ourselves too. And, all too often, the intention to try to pray slips.

We continue, perhaps, and find that much of prayer is not the passing experience which had encouraged us so much at first. Then to our subjective way of thinking, something else appears to be happening. And what is this? Does this activity, or state, or attitude have the constituent parts, or motive, which may allow us to say to ourselves that this is prayer, or that we have prayed?

You have often spoken and written of the absolute necessity for prayer in our lives, every day. What is this prayer? And, of course, here I am speaking of prayer as something distinct – when we are not doing any of the things which make us feel busy, unable to pray. These activities, please God, may be prayerful, be more prayerful than we know, but I mean those times when consciously, kneeling down, or still in a chair, we are saying 'No' to the many other things which we could be doing, trying to give that short time to Christ.

Can you say something about this which is very direct and assumes nothing about what I may, or may not, think about it all? And start at the beginning?

With much love,

   Mark

II Relationship the key

Dearest Mark,

You certainly don't give up! The occasion two summers ago is by no means the only time you have pushed me to the effort of writing of prayer. To my mind – and you know this – all I have written has been about prayer. In several places in my writings – I will quote chapter and verse if you want – I insist that prayer is essentially what God does in us not what we do. But you are right in saying that this assumes that my readers already pray; my words are a corrective of mistaken notions that hinder us not a little in our surrender to God.

However, I don't want to be pig-headed and so, here I am, really 'listening' to you and wanting sincerely to struggle, with you, to give some help to these questioners. You actually know them, feel with them and I listen to them through you. I know that for you the 'penny has dropped' and whatever your questioning mind fidgets with, you pray and in your deepest heart, underneath the conscious muddle and confusion, you know that you do, or rather I think the truth is that you know God well enough, the God revealed in Jesus, to be assured that it must be all right. How could this God, this love not be hearing your desire, seeing your effort, ignore you as you give time in your busy, busy life to be alone with Him? Unthinkable!

I suspect that something similar is true in many of those who, because they fail to grasp the sheer simplicity of prayer, go on looking for ways, for the answer, for some teacher as though prayer were a craft to be learned. The thing to do is to stop the roundabout, get off, sit on the ground, that is look into the ground, and pray. What I mean by the ground is one's own heart, one's own experience; listen to it.

'What is prayer?', that is your ruthless, insistent question. Is not the key word 'relationship'? Does not the mere idea, let alone the heart's instinctive need and desire presume relationship; that one, mysteriously, is in relation to, is not absolutely alone, somehow looked at, known, loved? Why would we want even subconsciously to contact, to make real this mysterious relationship to an Other – why even raise the question of prayer – unless at our core, in spite of emotional anxieties and doubts, this Other is assumed to care, to love us?

Aren't we saying that we know we are addressed? Of course, this is not obvious to our ordinary way of perceiving relationships and, if we are looking for it on that level (we do of course and it's the basis of our problem) we are off track. No, we have to reflect more deeply and admit to a dimension of ourselves that, though it expresses itself through ordinary, conscious experience yet is, I think we may say, independent of it. It is this dimension that will develop in prayer. But you know that this does not mean that we shall come to perceive it, become aware of it. How nice that would be! Of its very nature – it is where the divine, Holy Spirit 'dwells', communes – it cannot be available to our ordinary consciousness any more than can the holy One whose 'dwelling' it is. How important it is, Mark, for everyone to grasp that we have to fall back on images – for example, 'dwelling', to express the inexpressible and always remember that they are only images.

So, each of us in a relation, is a relation. This 'being addressed', being loved is what constitutes us. There is a real sense that, in seeking to pray, seeking the Other, we are seeking ourselves, finding out who we really are, seeking to be what we are and this is right, proper self-love, self-seeking, wholly one with seeking and loving God. We are created for this. It is to become human.

But it is essential, Mark, even at this preliminary stage of investigation, to assert emphatically that only in Jesus can we know the You who looks at me and says the 'you' that makes me the person I am. The great 'You' and the little 'you' can be known only in Jesus. Otherwise the 'You' is of our own making, a projection of our own mind and psyche and therefore within our control. We must, at the outset, consent to live in mystery and allow the You to reveal Itself and reveal who and what we are.

To sum up what I suggest is the ABC of praying: on our side it is a responding, an answering – You look at me, You call me. Here I am.

And further questions must follow: 'Who are You?' 'What must I do to receive You?' These last two questions will lead to the indispensable work of the mind in reading and reflecting on revelation.

With much love,

   Ruth

Very dear Ruth,

Thank you for your letter. You covered a lot of ground and gave me a lot to think about. Hence my delay in replying.

I pick out what you yourself put first, your insistence that 'prayer is essentially what God does in us, not what we do'. If the fundamental point is that the action which matters, is not ours, then any quest for a skill, or craft, the guru problem you touch on, really is an illusion, a search for security and achievement on our own terms. But such a fundamental point can be hard to remember unless it is made my own because the self freely assents, or even asserts, that it is true. This convinced sort of knowing that 'prayer is essentially what God does in us' must come from faith. Faith, as a gift, a proposition and a question, stood in capital letters behind every line of your letter.

What you say about being 'a relation', being 'addressed' is helpful in getting the basic ideas straight. But isn't there a situation or a stage which may precede this, a point of departure before faith really engages? I mean our early apprehension of transcendence, that gateway to realising that at first we seem alone. This realisation that the self has its own going on at different levels and, in a way, out of time, *may* emerge in response to a sense that some Other is beckoning, that there is a You who is calling me. I am not sure how common this is. I would guess that for many of us, the experience of transcendence is encountered in reverse gear as we feel detached from our dailiness and our cares, looking back at them, rather than as we launch out in a direction which is face forward towards something else. If you can see this, then you can understand a desire to pray, to reach out for a relationship, which is nonetheless weak in faith.

Of course, generalisations are very hard here. You say, later in your letter, that we are stuck with the problems of images. Yes – we do not know how to put what we know. What I am trying to say now is that difficulties in trying to pray may well come from weakness in faith. If both prayer and faith are not, to use the language of modern management, 'objectives' we can strive for in the expectation of achieving them, because they are properly the action of God, then how is the person to avoid a closed circuit of endeavour and disappointment? How may she or he break out, step into the humble acquiescence of letting God do what He has promised that He will do?

There is also an issue of faith in the proposition that the life of the spirit must be allowed to exist and develop 'beyond' what you call our 'ordinary consciousness'. Yes, how cosy and smug it would be if we could get some handle on this and track our developing spiritual life – a little more of this and a little less of that and we are set fair . . . The idea, however, that we must accept to go on without any assurance of seeing, never mind understanding, what is afoot, is a big challenge to faith.

You will quickly say that from the outset we must be clear about our motives. Is this a sincere turning to God, or an attempt to cultivate the self – what you say about 'our ordinary way of perceiving relationships'? My point about reversing into transcendence, rather than stepping out face forward, simply suggests that early on our motives may be hidden even from ourselves.

You may think that I am straying rather from the important 'fundamental ground'. But I know that you wrote your letter from a conviction which is suffused by faith and held up by it. Your communion with faith sets the scenery of human life in new perspectives which lead to a point on the horizon where faith must rest in the face mystery, living without expecting, or wishing, to resolve the absolute mystery of God's being in relation to, a relation of, us human beings. Thus you set your face towards the Father who is in Heaven, hidden but present in the heart of life.

And if this is not our daily reality, if faith has not yet rearranged our perceptions and expectations of life in this way; if we are trying to give religion a go because we are deeply unhappy, or just itchy about our dailiness; if we are trying to pray for a motive we may not fully be able to articulate, isn't our first prayer an asking for the gift of faith?

Your letter brings these abstracts squarely to the point. You say to our restlessness, 'Jesus'. Only in Jesus can we find answers to our questions, 'Who are You who is calling me forth from myself?' and 'Who am I that you are calling?' That is quite a jump, but at least it is a clear one. It makes me reflect how much we can assent to Christianity and the practice of religion without stopping to consider that fundamental point.

With much love,

   Mark

IV Seriousness about the natural ground of faith

Dearest Mark,

You are right, my ABC derives from faith. Of course it does, for I have no other viewpoint. I appreciate that it can seem to presume a lot, but not as much as it seems. The point I tried to make does not depend on faith, but I think it is the natural ground of faith and thus a stepping stone or an invitation to faith.

As I see it, it is a matter of simple logic and is commonplace. If a person wants to pray, surely that points to the fact that the person has at least an implicit assumption that there is Someone to pray to. I am asking that this assumption ('awareness' may be misleading) be looked at carefully, reflected upon. That is all. We are confining ourselves, aren't we, Mark, to this category of persons? I don't think we can allow ourselves to be diverted by questions regarding all the 'others'. We can happily leave them all to the God who loves each one with deathless fidelity.

I am repeating myself, I know, but I do feel it is important to pay attention to this 'experience'. We might ask: 'Why pray rather than dance or play the piano? What is the difference? Who do you want to contact? Why? Why not chat to a human friend instead?'

*I would hope that such questioning would induce a person
to reflect on the mysterious dimension whence such a strange
desire emerges; the 'heart' and the equally mysterious
assumption that there is Someone in touch, in relation to that
heart. To get people reflecting on this simple fact is, I believe,
to do them a great service. To begin to respond, consciously to
relate to this Someone, is the beginning of faith, faith which is
a gift, but a gift that must be prayed for, worked for, worked
with.*

*'If both prayer and faith are not, to use the language of
modern management, "objectives" we can strive for in the
expectation of achieving them, because they are properly the
action of God, then how is the person to avoid a closed circuit
of endeavour and disappointment?' You put your finger here,
Mark, on the underlying cause of all the 'problems' of prayer.
False, self-orientated expectations. Faith is not a game.
Discipleship of Jesus is not a game. We may not trivialise the
costly Gift of God. Of course, we can never judge but human
nature being what it is – a nature I too share – I fear that a
great deal of interest in 'prayer' has nothing or little to do
with the God who really is.*

*Here the mystery of individuals confronts us, of their
capacities, their freedom. I think that all we can do is direct
a person to Jesus, share with others what we ourselves
understand of the love of God, the seriousness of human life
and our eternal destiny, hoping that they will be motivated
towards true, selfless praying and, to quote you, 'break out,
step into the humble acquiescence of letting God do what He
has promised that He will do'.*

*We want them to base their lives on objective truth, on Jesus
who is Truth, and refuse to demand, to clutch at immediate
satisfaction, an appreciable pay-off. We know that there is a*

peace that only God can give, a joy that only God can give and 'not of this world'. If we talk here and now of the joys and satisfactions of prayer we offer base coinage. Prayer is, at bottom, the surrender of the whole self to God. It is genuine in the measure that the surrender is genuine and that must be our objective, not self-gratification.

Divine Love is always seeking the human heart, always knocking. You instance deep unhappiness, itchiness about our dailiness. Yes, and almost anything. It can be a real grief, can't it, to look on, recognise the One who is knocking and see the person either not hearing or disregarding what is really loving invitation. Once again, the mystery of human freedom.

I look forward to seeing you, Mark.

With my love

    Ruth

V Scripture

Very dear Ruth,

You speak of 'the indispensable work of the mind in reading and reflecting on revelation'. Yes, but there is a paradox for those who have been fortunate enough to have had Scripture as part of their upbringing. It can be so hard to get behind the familiar reactions set up so long ago, to read with a fresh eye. And perhaps, deep down, this is because we think we've done it – a parable starts . . . 'Oh yes, that one, I know how that one ends.' Well, if that's a difficulty, so be it. We have to face it and try to read again with the eye of the person we now think we are, recognising the child's eye which read so casually before.

Then you seem to be saying something I've not heard you say before. You speak of 'finding out who we really are . . . wholly one with seeking and loving God'. Are you saying Jesus will in fact disclose himself more deeply, even if indirectly, if we allow him to explore our own experience, rather than if we are trying always to reach his?

Is this what you mean by 'sit on the ground . . . and look . . . into one's own heart, one's own experience; listen to it'? If I have understood what you were saying, then say more about how we are actually to reflect on our experience and how this will only 'be known in Jesus'.

'The indispensable work of the mind' – in theology the mind is paired with faith. If there is work which will help our faith and so open us to prayer, what is it? Both faith, a virtue from God, and prayer, God's own action, are God's to give. It seems important to be dead clear about that bit which is ours to do, what we can do to be more ready to listen more attentively for his secret word.

With much love,

Mark

VI Faith and fidelity

Dearest Mark,

I propose to have ready for when you come, my response to the important point you raise, but in advance let me express it thus: you have heard me say over and over again that we must stand on objective truth not on our subjective feelings. And I have shown myself critical of teachings on prayer that give a great deal of significance to the subjective element in prayer, to what has been the person's conscious experiences during prayer. Yet in these letters I encourage a looking into the heart and paying attention to its experience, of discovering through prayer who we really are, of finding our true selves.

If I read you correctly, you express a certain problem with 'objective truth' as though it must, of its very nature, be 'out there'. Not so, of course. Rather, it must be, it is, my own truth, at the very centre of my heart, permeating my being.

With my love

    Ruth

VII Affirming objective truth

Dearest Mark,

I want to explain what I mean by making objective truth our own, bringing it down into our own heart. I will have to be personal and show how I use the gospel. I'll take what is immediately at hand, the gospel reading of today's Mass, John 14:1–7. The setting is, of course, the Last Supper, the audience are the disciples. Scriptural scholars could give me much information regarding the author's intention and his addressees, but for prayer I leave these aside. Jesus, the living One speaks here and now to me. He is that Someone to whom I am mysteriously related as discussed earlier. I don't have to imagine myself in the supper room or anything like that. Faith tells me that I can identify the someone of my heart with this Jesus who died and now is totally in God's dimension. I don't have to address him as 'out there', but as 'within' in deepest intimacy. I listen to the words, I pray to understand, to receive them as he wants me to, to know him truly, to allow myself to be transformed by him. The words are no longer mere words, they give me the living person. It isn't an intellectual exercise but a loving, faith-full receiving. It isn't a question of trying to squeeze out of myself some feeling response, evoke some powerful realisation but a humble decision to stake my life on Jesus, not on mere religious feeling and intuitions. 'I am the way, the truth and the life', this Lord says to me and I want to take those words with absolute seriousness and live my life from them, on them, by them.

*Generalisations are misleading but perhaps I can venture that
very roughly we can divide those who pray into two
categories: those from whose psyche arise religious emotion,
intuitions, intimations of one kind or another; those whose
psyche remains impervious to such and who must depend on
their minds alone. There is a danger of the first too quickly
assuming that they have a keen faith. They feel they have. The
test comes when their psyche is dry and totally unresponsive.
Do they persist in prayer, all the same? The second may well
feel that their faith is non-existent. The same test must be
applied: do they pray on? What all of us have to grasp and try
to hold to consistently is that the One we are relating to is too
great for our human mind and heart. We must hold to this even
at times when we seem nearly to touch the divine; we must
hold to this when we are faced with a blank, a nothing, a
disheartening silence. Faith is independent of both states of
feeling.*

*I wonder if you see, Mark, how real faith is that dying to self
and to this world that the New Testament is constantly taking
about? You know how, at the Easter Vigil, when candidates are
asked to be baptised or we, to renew our baptismal promises,
are asked questions: 'Do you believe . . . ?' and we answer, 'I
do.' Baptism is the sacrament that expresses faith, conversion,
that fundamental change of heart that Jesus called for. Paul
understands baptism, for that very reason, as a going down
into death, into the tomb with Jesus and rising to new life in
him. I believe in God, the Father Almighty, in Jesus Christ, His
only Son, our Lord, etc. I like the old way of saying I believe
'on' because that gives the idea that we are no longer standing
on the same ground. Now we are grounded not in this world,
the world of merely human perception, bounded by limitation
but have leaped into, been carried into the realm of absolute
Reality that alone gives meaning to what we perceive by our
natural powers, as real, including ourselves. But this absolute*

Reality to which we surrender cannot be tested, cannot be proved. Faith is the divine enablement to stake our lives on what is invisible, untestable. As I have often said, Mark, I know I could never affirm this Reality apart from Jesus. His faith is my faith.

In the gospel text I have taken we have Jesus urging us to go on believing and trusting no matter what. 'Believe in God, believe in me, yes, even when you see me defeated, abandoned.' And the evangelist deliberately puts these words on Jesus' lips on the very eve of his terrible passion and death which the disciples will witness and their faith will be tested to the uttermost. I have always seen that fidelity to prayer is the most clear affirmation of faith or expression of faith. It simply makes no sense whatever if 'it isn't true'. It is sheer nonsense and a waste of time. It may often feel that 'it isn't true', but to persist in prayer is faith at its purest. Real prayer is real faith. Of course faith has and must have many expressions and there are many occasions when faith is put to the test more dramatically, more excruciatingly, but still, fidelity to prayer day in, day out, has a special purity.

This letter is too long already, but you will surely see that faith shows us something of who and what we are, our deepest meaning, besides which all we think we know about ourselves or that any science affords us, seems trivial.

I will ask Anna to put this letter in The Hermitage so that it will be there for you after Mass. But it doesn't matter if you haven't read it before we meet as we have heaps to talk about already. Until then,

With my love,

> *Ruth*

VIII A knowledge which is lived

Very dear Ruth,

Thank you for my visit. A couple of days' silence were a great rest and mercy. It was lovely to see you and thank you for the time you gave me.

Just now I want to reflect for a moment on what you have said so far. One of the best things you said during my visit, when I was having a go at you about the 'simplicity of prayer' was in a low voice, 'I never said it was easy.' Give me a moment then to catch up with what you have written so far. Can I try to summarise?

'Prayer is essentially what God does in us, not what we do.' This is the foundation and if we keep returning to this, we remember not to try to rely too much on ourselves or to keep testing our own reactions. You then insist on the simple point that if we have some sense of being addressed, then there is a You who is calling us, and that this You loves us. 'Who are You?' 'What must I do to receive You?' These are questions to which we can only find answers in the person of Jesus.

The fact of our desire to respond to this mysterious dimension itself deserves careful reflection; and this is the beginning of faith. The object of faith can be familiar from our upbringing and knowledge of religion, but true faith which is the element, the essence, of true prayer turns towards the God who is – the God who is greater and more mysterious than we can comprehend.

The true God whom you could never affirm as Reality apart from Jesus, is to be encountered in the heart – the deepest recesses of the soul's self. It is here that His truth is revealed in its actual import for me, the person this You addresses. And this truth is first given to us in the teaching of Jesus, in the word of revelation. It can become 'my truth', that ground on which 'I stand' in my life, by allowing it honestly and without reservation to explore and take possession of my natural resistance to it.

In this there is some dying, not only to the world, but to the self, as we surrender parts of ourselves to this truth and allow ourselves to be transformed by it – in the heart, a real conversion which accepts the action of God, prayer – which God does, not ourselves.

Now is that all right? Is that a fair summary, allowing for compression and untidiness, of the main themes you have put forward so far?

As you spotted, I have found the most difficult part of this the idea of possessing truth, making it my own. I think I had a resistance to this out of an inhibition about assuming for myself that I could have some freehold on truth. I can now see (if I have not misunderstood you) that you have in mind the result of allowing the Word to work away at the self. This result would not be something I have acquired, in the sense of an object that could be disposed of, but a change of heart which is mine because it has happened in me. Such a change is likely to be small, but it could be inalienably mine if welcomed and allowed to grow.

A second difficulty in this is keeping clear of the idea of intellectual truth. Most of the intellectual truths we hold are limited in scope. We may well find it easier to defend them in daily life – for instance the clear injustice of an instance of racial or sexual discrimination. Perhaps this is because they do not impinge very deeply or broadly in an ordinary and conventional life. So they are easier to handle.

The truth you speak of is inseparable from the Truth. It permeates the heart and triggers reflex admissions of obligation and assent which may well be inconvenient and unwelcome to personality just as much as intellect. This is truth of a different order and challenging in a different way. The defences of the selfish self run deeper than we allow and are never more agile than in influencing the arguments of the mind, shifting the ground back to the easier terrain of intellectual understanding.

Lastly, there is the difficulty of remembering that, in this necessarily interior language of self and heart, the first and last words are the God who loves us, 'a Divine Love who is always seeking the human heart'. It is easy to evade this, to transfer focus too quickly to what we think we must do next, to those obligations to others to which we never seem to measure up. And this is competing against a standard which surreptitiously we are in fact setting for ourselves. There may not be a malicious vanity here, but there is a vanity all the same. Isn't one of the big barriers to prayer our inhibition about accepting the love Jesus has for each one of us as we are?

Sister Wendy, in her introduction to your *Living in Mystery* wrote of 'a living knowledge not so much felt as lived'. What an enormous gulf separates an intellectual apprehension from a knowledge which is lived and gets into the practical detail of ordinary life, is plain as the daylight by which we live. The gulf is as great as the difference we know between what we resist as a threat and what we reach out for as a support without which life would be unimaginable.

The other thing you said when we met which took hold, was about the seriousness of prayer. 'When we see how much faith matters to another, why don't we ask, "Well, why doesn't it matter like that to me?".' That is a marvellous question. We all know the easy answers, like 'Because I haven't got that sort of faith.' I think if I take a few minutes to reflect deeper on that question, I find my way towards much of what you have written.

Thank you again for the visit. It was splendid to see you.

With much love,

    Mark

IX The test of charity

Dearest Mark,

If it isn't condescending to say so. I think you give a fine, lucid summary of where we have got so far.

Even to see the gulf between intellectual knowledge and real knowledge is grace. How easily it is assumed that because we see something to be true, have an intellectual understanding of it, we really know it. Really to know it is, as you realise, for it to become 'my truth', not as a possession but as something that has possessed me and is affecting my whole life. Let me illustrate. I find now that, among spiritual people, 'spiritual poverty' is much talked about. One can read lyrical passages on the subject, listen to persons talking sincerely enough of their experience of poverty and yet it is obvious that it is not a reality, merely an idea and a beautiful, appealing, 'spiritual' idea. Whereas the reality, in fact, is most unbeautiful, cannot be easily talked about so repulsive is it humanly speaking and only light from the naked, 'emptied' Jesus can reveal its beauty. One can witness the very people who know all about poverty, as soon as the real thing comes their way, reacting violently, finding all sorts of escape routes from what they are convinced cannot be of God.

Don't we get a lot of talk about Christian charity, concern for the Third World and those underprivileged in any way? This is fine provided it springs from a heart really committed to others in loving self-sacrifice and is not a cover for resentment towards authority, to a certain class of persons, or is not an expression of self-assertiveness and self-importance. The test will always be at 'home'. In this humdrum, irritating, perhaps ego-demeaning situation are we equally concerned to love, understand, show tolerance, salve wounds? It is in this 'home' situation that our ego gets its knocks, its thwartings and its chance to abdicate. We are only beginning to understand the love Jesus asks of us when we prefer, choose the welfare, the easing of others to our own and especially when we receive no obvious reward, no thanks or appreciation.

With my love,

Ruth

Very dear Ruth,

Having put some of the groundwork ideas in place, can we
link them to what may be the common experience – a personal
practice of prayer which possibly hasn't developed much since
early in life? We may feel very awkward with prayer because
we realise that our approach to prayer is dislocated from adult
experience. It's like trying to speak in a foreign language when
you are a beginner: here are kind, interested and interesting
foreigners and all you can say in very simple language is how
long you have been in the country, ask how many children
they have, and so on. We don't seem to be able to pray where
we are, or, more subtly, where we feel we are.

Our earliest memories are possibly of petitionary prayer,
asking God for what we want. I think now of somebody the
other day who told me that she would like to pray more, but
she found herself only asking for things for herself and felt a
bit guilty about this – it seemed so selfish – and so by and
large she didn't pray, though she would like to, and so on . . .
This was an expression of how close we can come to prayer
and then veer off. Like a hawk in the air, looking intently, but
then sweeping sideways on the wind, we are caught for a bit
and then go away.

If I feel the wind is high and I am having real difficulty in
paying any attention to what I am doing, constantly tempted to

slip down the wind, I find that asking prayer is a good way of holding on to something. What do you think about petitionary prayer?

With much love,

    Mark

XI Desire and motive in prayer

Dearest Mark,

Of course I did not meet your lady and, had I done so, might well feel differently, but in the abstract, I find her attitude the very antithesis of seriousness. One would think that, whether she chooses to pray or not is on a par with, let's say, choosing whether to take up painting or sewing. I recall – it must be forty years ago – a diocesan priest asking if I would 'adopt' him in a special way by praying for him. He went on to say that, during his time in the seminary, he wasn't, like some, attracted to prayer and so did not 'take it up'. This was said without a hint of self-reproach or even regret, but merely as a statement of fact. Prayer wasn't a necessity, just a hobby to be taken up if one was so inclined or left aside if not. Seemingly I was to do his praying for him.

This lady is accurate in her use of the term 'like' rather than 'want'. Only too often you hear people say they want to pray but . . . If we want a thing we go for it; we show that we want it and not merely feel we would like it, by taking trouble to get it. If we want to pray, we pray.

Mark, would not this friend reflect that the very fact that she asks for things, even for herself, is an admission that there is Someone there to ask? It is because she has not so reflected that she remains in this poised, uncommitted state. The Someone hasn't enough reality for her. This, in my opinion, saving a remarkable grace of God, is for her the basic step: reflection on that Presence. Then, I hope, she would be led to

*reflect on Jesus Christ. I cannot see how otherwise she can
escape from this frightened self-centredness and from the
dissatisfaction and sense of guilt she feels.*

*There are two important issues involved in your letter: the lack
of seriousness and the prayer of petition. I feel this latter must
have a separate treatment. I need space to reflect more on this
vital subject. So hold up your response to this letter until you
gets its sequel, hopefully in about a week's time. But before
closing, I want to hark back to the main topic of this one,
namely the need for great seriousness. I was moved, Mark, by
what you said when you were here. We were talking over the
mystery of why some people 'wake up' to God, so to speak,
and others – we had in mind really good people – do not. You
felt that a choice had to be made more or less in the dark, with
little conscious impulse, to take God seriously. It was when you
made up your mind to get up an hour earlier each morning to
go to Mass ensuring that you had fifteen minutes prayer either
before or after, that, quoting you, you 'got hooked'. And I
know how you use, economise on time to read books that
nourish your faith. I agree with you. God does not do for us
what we can do for ourselves. You have wanted and go on
wanting and this is expressed practically in choices and often
costly ones. I cannot see that there is any other way forward.
I hope you are satisfied with what I have written in response
to your letter, but hold on, even if not. You will hear again
shortly.*

With my love,

    Ruth

Dearest Mark,

*Isn't Christian existence itself petition, or even, leaving
Christianity aside, religious existence in general? It is the
expression of dependency; of the awareness of our limitation
and helplessness in so many areas. One doesn't need to have
lived long to know this by experience. But staying within our
own context of Christianity, petition, asking is the practical
admission that we are here to receive, to be 'done unto' and
the deeper our faith the more we know that this is pure
blessedness. We are here to receive all that God, divine Love
has to give. The Church's liturgical prayer is almost all an
asking. Even the acts of praise reveal that we depend on divine
aid to enable us to praise: God must praise God within us.
Personally, I have difficulty with assertions that praise, 'pure
adoration' is the highest form of prayer. I feel unable to praise,
not big enough to praise; I do not know God enough to burst
into praise. But surely humble petition, the awareness of
need and confidently exposing that need to God is praise,
is adoration? Isn't it glorifying God's love? I think so. I feel
praise, of itself, a bit presumptuous. That's a personal
idiosyncrasy, I know, and spiritual people think otherwise. I
always ask Jesus to praise for me because he knows, he sees
and what is more he is the praise and glory of the Father.
'Through him, with him, in him is to You Eternal Father, in
the unity of the Holy Spirit, all honour and glory for ever and*

ever, Amen.' That I understand. So you see, Mark, I am all for petitionary prayer.

However, all the above assumes much. It is not our normal human experience. This vision of faith does not 'beat in our pulses', does not shine in our minds in such a way as to compel attention and enrapture our hearts. Our daily experience is of our needs, our anxieties and concerns here and now. We are concerned about those we love, their health, their well-being; concerned may be about continuing in employment; about our children, their progress in school on which their future seems to depend; who of us is not in close contact with someone in affliction of mind or body? These are the things that press on our hearts and that we pray about. No Christian could possibly deny the validity of such prayer. Look at the gospels: 'Lord, if you want to, you can make me clean'; 'Lord, come and heal my child'; 'Lord, he whom you love, is sick.' Our Lord made people see that he was there for them, there to be asked, there to help and there to heal. We get Paul and others exhorting their communities to lay their needs before God, lay bare their anxieties, cast their cares on the Lord, intercede for others.

We go to God, pray to God, as we are, where we are. Two people could be saying the same words, making the same petition but one has a heart purely directed to God, full of faith and love, the other a heart still harbouring a great deal of selfishness. 'Son, they have no wine', Jesus' mother could say. 'Lord, please make my party a success', another could plead because she hates losing face before others. God loves us as we are, where we are and will always be intent on drawing us on. God does not despise us in our weakness, in our small notions of love.

As you say, Mark, I expect for most of us who had the good fortune to be brought up in a Christian environment, petitionary prayer was our first introduction to prayer. It was certainly mine. Family night prayers held a list of petitions: God bless mother and father, my brother and sisters, all aunts and uncles . . . Still, the programme was headed by the Our Father, Hail Mary and Glory be to the Father, as well as an act of contrition. I remember that we prayed for the holy souls. We would pray for a fine day for our picnic, to pass our exams, as well as for a neighbour who was sick. 'Ordinary' folk in those days would not know how to pray otherwise than by using set prayers. I know my father and mother knelt down morning and evening to 'say' their prayers. I am sure many of these centred on us children. But what mattered was their hearts. They gave time to this, they were expressing faith and trust; they were looking for guidance. Divine Love, I am certain, was entering their hearts, purifying, enlightening them and making them grow in faith and love even though they may not have been aware of it. Here I would repeat my basic insight regarding prayer, that it is not what we do but what God does in us. Petitionary prayer is our way of keeping in touch with God in our daily lives and what we are really doing is ensuring that God's help is there for us to endure with patience and love whatever befalls.

So, to return to your lady. She was praying for herself only and came to see that this was selfish. Why not believe this awareness was grace, God's response? To see our selfishness is grace. The sad part is that she packs up. God wants her to pray to be less selfish, to be shown how to be better. And if she cannot sincerely want that, then to pray to want it, to want to want. But pray. Go on addressing that Someone. If I were in contact with her I would like to suggest that she made a little choice, namely to take ten minutes each day to recite the Our Father slowly, pondering on what it might mean, wanting what it wants, which is what Jesus saw God wants for us, identifying

*this Father with that Someone she asked things of. I would
urge her to persevere in this whether she likes it or not, gets
anything out of it or not, no matter how wooden it all seemed.
But I think that you, Mark, could suggest she might read
something to develop her knowledge of Jesus and the Father to
whom he prays. There is no way round this taking of trouble.
She must choose. She must do what she can. But we need one
another, Mark, and we must not be afraid of offering a helping
hand, sharing our own insight as best we can.*

*To conclude, I have little time with all the attempts to explain
how intercessory prayer 'works'. My mind is rational enough
and such questions naturally arise, but I ignore them. It is
enough for me that Jesus tells us to ask, to seek, to knock.
We see him making petitions; the Our Father is petition
throughout. That is enough for me and I leave the whole thing
in its mystery. I know God is all love, that no sigh, no prayer
goes unanswered and this includes our most earthly and,
maybe selfish prayers as well as those that are truly 'in my
name'; wholly according to the mind of Jesus. How, in what
way, I leave to God.*

With my love,

  Ruth

Dearest Mark,

Here is a copy of a recent exchange of letters with a friend.
I'm sending them to you because in my reply I've written some
of the things which I think are important about prayer.

> *Dear Sister,*
> *I have thought long and hard about how to express my difficulties in*
> *prayer. The general discussions we have had over some time have*
> *helped me greatly, but I still have a nag and it is something like this.*
>
> *In the past I used to be able, I thought, to meditate but now seem*
> *to have a block: emptying my mind so that God can communicate*
> *with me rather than my putting thoughts into His mind, is proving*
> *hopeless. I find it difficult to reach an 'empty' state and all that*
> *happens is I get frustrated and disturbed.*
>
> *I have also been worried that while I appear to be able to think and*
> *talk to Our Lord at odd times during the day, regular periods of*
> *prayer become sterile and irritating.*
>
> *I think I can guess largely how you will answer this from the*
> *discussions we have had and from what you write in your books,*
> *but somehow I need an extra word or shove or something to rid*
> *me of the nag.*
>
> *If you could say something to me, Sister, about these things I would*
> *be most grateful.*
>
> *With Love*
>
> *Pat*

Dear Pat

Many thanks for you thoughtful letter. Certainly I will try to help you. The fact that we have talked together several times makes it easier.

Where on earth did you pick up the idea that you must empty your mind to receive God? If from me, then you have misunderstood me. St Teresa, that great contemplative, states roundly that God gave us our minds to work with and so we must use them. She is protesting against a teaching, current in her day – does it ever go away? – that, ideally in the life of prayer, the time must come when thought should be laid aside, even reflection on Jesus' humanity, and one strives, by some sort of spiritual elevation, to reach 'pure God'. Teresa abhors the notion. She sees it as presumptuous, a lack of humility, an assumption that we can raise ourselves to God by our own powers. I see it as striking at the very heart of the gospel, as I will show.

Now I know one hears a lot today of the advantages to be had from the techniques of Zen and other Eastern disciplines. I do not want to get involved in this subject about which I know little anyway. I mention it just because it seems to hold allure for many good and earnest people. Or rather, I suspect, that it sounds so 'spiritual', so very much the 'thing', what one would expect union with God to involve, that therefore one ought to go for it. But just to be practical: 'emptying the mind' calls for enormous, concentrated effort, and this takes a great deal of time. Thus it is open only to the few with the leisure and the degree of intelligence it needs. This fact alone warns us off. The way of true prayer is open to all, the clever and simple, the busy and people of leisure, rich and poor and so forth and so forth.

I am a Christian and a Catholic and humbly acknowledge that to me has been given the unspeakable grace of knowing Jesus Christ, my Lord. You, dear Pat, can claim the same privilege. We need no other way for he is our Way, our Teacher, our All. Just look at the New Testament. There is nothing whatever to suggest that praying demands mysterious techniques, is open only to a privileged few. There it is taken for granted that prayer is as natural to the human spirit as breathing is to the body. Jesus talks directly about communing with 'your Father in heaven . . . ', praying in secret to this One who knows every movement of the heart, listens to its longings with tender love and rewards them. What other reward than the gift of the divine Self? This is the good news, the unbelievably good news. The God revealed in Jesus is pure compassion, pure unconditional Love offered to every single one of us. The priceless Gift is there for all, continually on offer and all anyone has to do is to say, 'Yes.'

We say our 'Yes' in all sorts of ways, whenever, in fact, we do God's will, but our present concern is with the time devoted exclusively to prayer. This is the privileged moment of 'Yes' because it contains nothing else – no good work, nothing that gives earthly justification. It is a very pure act of faith in the God of Jesus and not in a God of human devising. In effect we are saying: 'I offer you nothing but myself here to receive You. I believe utterly, through Jesus, that You are here for me, at this very moment giving Yourself to me. I believe Your word against all my feelings, all that "seems" to me. I stake everything on You, Jesus' Abba.'

That is the fundamental attitude needed for prayer: faith that God acts now, in me; that prayer has all to do with God, not with me precisely; with what God does, not with my performance. You have begun to realise this and I smiled at your way of expressing it. I am convinced that all our problems with prayer, our worries, our fidgets, derive from lack of faith. We do not look at Jesus and the Father he reveals, but only on a God of human projection and this God is terribly difficult to find, very complicated, very puzzling, but also, be it noted, this God gives me a great deal to do, makes me feel, however secretly, very important spiritually. Our Father shows us our littleness, our nothingness, our helplessness and we don't like it.

Reflecting on all this I recalled my childhood and the great event of putting on a Christmas play for our parents. How important we were, busy writing our script, making costumes, fitting up a corner of the sitting room as a stage, fairy lights attached to the curtain rail. Come Christmas evening, armchairs were put in the opposite corner and our parents duly conducted thereto and solemnly handed a programme with dramatis personae. Then such loving appreciation and applause with the unfailing accolade from our father: 'The only thing wrong with it is that it is too short; let's have it all over again.' But, heavens above! What were our frolics achieving for the government of the world, even for paying the household bills? It was our parents who were doing the important things, things that really matter: looking after our health and well-being, arranging our schooling and so on. All they asked of us was just to be who we were, their children whom they could love and be good to. Our play was telling them in its own child language that we loved them very much, wanted to give them pleasure. I feel that is the situation in prayer in regard to what we do. God is happy with whatever we do provided we let Him love us and be good to us. What we do has really no more significance than our Christmas play. What God is looking at and sees infallibly is the heart's intent. What am I really wanting? I think our principal 'work' at prayer must be faith in God's wonderful love and begging, by our staying at prayer if not with implicit acts, to believe, to be purified of all that prevents God loving us to His heart's content.

Do you know, I think it is best to leave it at that. I could go on to answer your query more directly, but I feel it is not necessary and perhaps unwise. You are very intelligent. 'She that has ears to hear let her hear.' You have heard it all before, read it in my books, but none of us can overdo recalling, rehearing it. I am confident that, pondering what I have written, you will apply it to yourself and know the answers. Each of us is unique and I feel it is far better to give the theology, the deep principles of prayer, than to start suggesting how an individual might conduct herself or himself at prayer.

But perhaps I could make one more general point and one that is, in practice, very difficult for us to accept, namely that distractions do not matter and we ought not to spend a lot of energy trying to avoid them. Were we to think we should make that effort, that would mean that we insisted on taking control of our prayer and we must not do this. Distractions are inevitable simply because our mind is made to think thoughts and will do its job almost as automatically as the stomach digests food. The only way to control it would be to give it its proper food, that is plenty of God-thoughts, but by your own admission these no longer help you at prayer time and you are right not to employ them except insofar as you are drawn to do so and as they foster the basic attitude of receptivity I have tried to explain to you. All any of us can do is turn away from our distractions when we are aware of them and reaffirm our intention of being there for Our Lord. Even if at the end of the period for prayer you realise that most of it has been passed lost in distractions, the great thing is to refuse to worry, just cast yourself into God's arms and tell Him that even though your gaze has turned away from Him, His has not turned

*from you and that He has continued to love you and give himself to
you. I am confident that what God is concerned with is our intention
and this remains stable, doesn't it?*

*Still, if you are not satisfied, do not hesitate to write again and never
think it is a trouble for me. What can be more important, more of a
privilege than to help someone grow into true prayer?*

*Experiencing a happy freedom in our intercourse with God, Our
Lord, during the day in contrast to the difficulty, the hang-up we
have during our prayer time itself, is a common experience. I suggest
that there are two ways of looking at it. The first is that going about
our daily tasks, doing things as we must, gives our faculties their
proper function. They are happy. This means that we are not
harassed by their restlessness and we find it easy to direct our
thoughts frequently to prayer. I believe that the use of the rosary,
litanies of a repetitive nature and even the 'Jesus prayer' are
'methods' based on this psychological wisdom. Not infrequently,
whilst the mind is partially employed in the words, the mysteries
indicated, a deeper dimension is exposed to God's loving
communication. This is wonderful and I believe thousands of
people have been sanctified in this way of praying. Of course, like
everything else, methods can become substitutes for real prayer, acts
to be accomplished, a quota of devotions to be got through.*

*The other point is not universally applicable but I am confident that in
your case, it is so: namely that it is precisely fidelity to time of prayer,
to the remaining exposed in that often disconcerting, 'unsatisfactory'
way before God, that enables this facility, ensures that you really do
try to live for God, do all you do through Him, with Him and in Him.
The great mistake people make and, alas, I have known Carmelites
themselves succumb, is to abandon the times for 'unoccupied' prayer
because 'I can pray much better when I am doing something quiet,
gardening for instance'.*

*Be very little before God, very trusting and happy. Do not try to do
what you cannot do. Do not exasperate yourself and drive yourself to
frustration. Just be you and keep offering yourself to Love. You will
pray for me, won't you? This comes with my love and my prayers.*

   Ruth

Very dear Ruth,

Your letter to Pat contains the hard but vital piece of advice
you once gave to me, 'The great mistake people make . . . is to
abandon the times for unoccupied prayer.' That's the heart of
it. You make me ask again what is this prayer and why do we
find that in practice we avoid it? Why do we make this 'great
mistake'?

I want to try to avoid jargon, setting up some special vocabulary
for sorting out the different strands of what we mean, but by
'unoccupied prayer', you seem to be pointing at what I guess
many people would really mean by 'prayer'. And why is this?
Why do we make a distinction which I think you yourself
would not make?

Perhaps for most lay people the usual experience of prayer is
in the liturgy. And so it is primarily vocal and participatory.
We go to Mass on Sundays. There will be moments of
silent prayer, not least in the Eucharistic prayer around the
consecration, but these are moments and part of the mind
will be very aware of what's coming next, when it will
be time to stand up again. The event of going to Mass, the
church setting and the fact of the holy Presence in the
tabernacle and at the altar, all these work their influence.
The chameleon in us is content with this background. The
powerful benefits of habit are released. And we think this is

different from another sort of prayer (what you mean by
unoccupied prayer) because it is familiar; because we have
had a lot of catechism about it; because we are not alone.
That other sort which is not liturgical, is not so familiar. It
is open country which we do not know, where we may fear
to get lost and where, critically – and what a crisis it can
be – we feel alone.

There are immediate things to be said now about faith and the
horses in your mind are probably pulling to get them out. But
hold on to them for a moment because there is something else
I want you to look at first. The important argument is about
faith. It is the key issue, but even those who see this, do need
something for the mind at first as well.

I was struck by what Hans Urs von Balthazar wrote in his
book, *Prayer* (p. 97):

> Some lay people, with a view to taking a more sustained part in
> the liturgy of the Church, follow, to some extent, the manner of life
> and prayer of priests and monks, and say the daily Office either in
> whole or in part. But, in general, they have less understanding and
> spiritual freedom than those who, in the less formalised practice of
> contemplative prayer, allow God's life that is in them to illuminate
> their way. The former practice may be recommended in exceptional
> cases, but, for most people, it is a mistaken one.

My reaction to this was that von Balthazar was touching on
the resistance most have to 'unoccupied' prayer and suggesting
that lay people must not avoid this motive for resistance, but
face it directly. Their response to the gift of a desire to pray
should not be channelled into what could easily deteriorate
into another 'activity', another form of social inclusion.
They should consider the gift, reflect on it, in the silence of
themselves, reaching out for the conviction that they are not
alone.

I think this advice from von Balthazar could seem shocking. I wonder if you can see how powerfully magnetic for the laity inclusion in the Church can be? The good, necessary and important aspects of that pull are obvious, but there is also an undertow which I see as simply deriving from our political natures, from the fact that people are gregarious and also at root selfish, worrying about how they fit in. And that undertow seems to me to run against prayer.

In prayer and unoccupied prayer we have the chance to own up to these anxieties and to place them in the hands of Christ. We can do so without fear or inhibition. In private prayer he gives us the confidence even to find and hand over the bits we had kept back, even to accept with good humour some of the facts about ourselves which are, in this life, inescapable elements in our own make up. My own experience is that this is the ground, the silent hard earth, in which faith first grows. 'Painfully you will get your food from it' (Genesis 3:17).

These are the reasons which, looking back, have made more and more sense to me of your advice that private, unoccupied prayer cannot be left out and why I noticed so quickly the same thought in your letter. I wonder if this makes sense to you.

With much love,

    Mark

XV Personhood and self-surrender

Dearest Mark,

You raise an interesting – better, an important – question. What von Balthazar writes, does on the face of it, seem shocking but both of us see that he has a point. You are in a far better position than I to verify or refute it. What we can say with certainty is that no one may predict just how God will work, what means He will use to bring each and all to himself. No two people are identical, each has her or his unique relationship with God and God can and will guide the person, provided there is cooperation. Assuming that basic premise but leaving it aside for the moment, I think we must confront the issue in a general sort of way. At the root of it lie two inseparable, interacting, interdependent aspects of our Christian being, and they, of course, as everything else in our Christian being, have their roots in nature: solitariness and community.

Each of us is a unique, irreplaceable person, but uniquely, most truly and fully a person only in relationship to other similarly unique persons: in 'communion'. A community is something quite different from a group of people sharing common interests. Community, in the Christian sense, does not just happen, it is brought about by the Holy Spirit. The more fully each individual surrenders to this Holy Spirit, is controlled by Him, so is community really community. Works of charity, loving service, neighbourliness, all these indeed are

vital, but of themselves do not create a Christian community.
Our communion must be at the deepest level of being.

This must preface my attempt to answer your own shrewd
observation, ' . . . how powerfully magnetic for the laity
inclusion in the Church can be . . . the undertow which I see as
simply deriving from our political natures, the fact that people
are gregarious and also at root selfish, worrying about how
they fit in. And that undertow seems to me to run against
prayer'.

Earlier you observe how easily reciting the Office and even
participation in the Mass can deteriorate into another
'activity'. You are implying, if not stating baldly, that
Christians in this instance are attending to one aspect of our
Christian reality and neglecting the other. Insofar as this is so,
then community and communal prayer are impoverished.
Whatever appears, there cannot be real community. 'That they
may all be one; even as You, Father, are in me and I in You,
that they also may be one in Us' (John 17:21).

This shows the need for what we are calling 'unoccupied
prayer'. What is this prayer? I shall attempt an answer, but
must grope for words. Leaving aside all other occupation and,
in intention, mental preoccupation, this 'me' (I shrink from
saying 'I' as it seems self-assertive) 'looks at', 'comes before',
'encounters' the living God. Unoccupied prayer is equally
undefended prayer. This 'me' is exposed to God, stripped of
pretension, naked, refusing comforting make-believe and
offering itself to be gazed at, searched out and seen in total
reality by the God who, in Jesus, we know to be Absolute Love.
Power, holiness, justice – whatever other attributes we impute
to the God are nothing but expressions of God's nature as
Love. It is Love that is almighty, unutterable holiness,
supremely just, and so forth. 'Fear not!' And this Love has the

special quality of compassion, tender understanding and loving acceptance of us in all our sinfulness.

We can't disgust God. We might get fed up. God is never fed up, but always delights in us. So we can afford to be undefended and want this Love to enter every corner of our being because only then will everything in us be purified and transformed. When we pretend to ourselves and therefore to God, and when we are out to impress – ourselves first of all, but also God – with whatever holy sentiments, great desires or profound spirituality we think we have, God can't get at us! Again, we can arm ourselves with a plan of prayer we intend to carry through in order to make sure we don't get distracted for that, of course, would be to fail. What is more, we absolutely dread the awareness of how spiritually inadequate we really are and our ego takes subtle precautions to ward it off. The common dodge is to avoid altogether this undefended prayer. And this is understandable enough without faith in Jesus' God.

This God longs and longs to give, not just gifts, but himself; and it is only this supreme Gift that make us utterly happy. We don't have to bribe Him with our good works or make ourselves desirable and 'worthy'. His love makes us lovely. The little story of Martha and Mary expresses the truth graphically. What Jesus is saying is that, when he enters our house, that is, when we are in direct contact with him, then it is for him to give to us, to serve and feed us, not the other way round. This, I believe, represents the reality of Christian existence: receiving God, All-Love, in Christ, letting God love us, nourish us, bring us to our total fulfilment. Well nourished, we turn to our neighbours and share our nourishment with them. Freely we have received and freely we must give.

It is hard for us to hold onto this underlying truth. We turn it upside down, don't we? This is where I see the utmost *importance of the prayer we are talking about: it expresses this truth as nothing else does. The Martha in us who wants to do things for God, wants to be the big one, the giver, must let go and childlike sit down with Mary at the feet of Jesus to receive. In doing so, her attitude will gradually change and her whole life, her serving, be purged of self-seeking and become in itself prayer. Our inmost heart must choose to remain a little one receiving its food from Jesus.*

It is not easy to persevere faithfully in this solitary, defenceless prayer. We can be faced with seeming nothingness. What we have to realise is that the silence, the emptiness, if such be our experience, are filled with a love too great for human heart and mind to grasp. They are what seems, not what is.

Faith tells us that Love works and Its work is Love. We have but to stay there in quiet trust, even if we suffer. This is not to say that methods are barred. Yet they must be used with a light touch and not become a screen behind which we hide our spiritual impotence. Their purpose must be to help us to maintain our undefended aloneness before our God.

It is this direct encounter of the Christian with her or his Creator and Lover that above all else creates personhood. We are not born persons in the true sense; we become persons through encounter with others, but supremely through direct encounter with God in Jesus. The two encounters are inseparable. We cannot encounter the human other in a profound way unless we are exposed to the Divine Other; but equally, unless we encounter in love the human person whom we see, we cannot encounter in love, the God we cannot see (cf. 1 John 4:20).

Simply because we are social animals, essentially fearful, we shrink from solitary exposure. We may be using liturgical prayer as a protective screen and our tactic is effectively concealed from ourselves by liturgy's sacred character. Though in reality we are participating in something bigger than ourselves, nevertheless, we know how to do it; there are clear directives and, moreover, we are supported by others. I think von Balthazar is right to suggest a danger and you to take it up. No one can possibly judge for another or others that participation in liturgy is, in fact, an alibi. We must appraise ourselves, no one else.

I don't want to end by giving the impression that the sort of prayer we are discussing is necessarily bleak. At times it might be enrapturing. The point I want to emphasise is the unprotectedness, the naked exposure to 'the length, the breadth, the height, the depth' of reality which is the love of God that comes to us in Christ Jesus Our Lord. We are, each one, enfolded in a love so overwhelming that it escapes conception. 'As a child has rest on its mother's breast / Even so my soul' (Psalms 131:2). ' . . . And he took them in his arms, and blessed them, laying his hands upon them' (Mark 10:16).

Our faith is not likely to be challenged at such depth when we are engaged with others in liturgical prayer. It seems to me that this unoccupied prayer is faith at its purest, refusing to stand on our own perception and casting our whole weight on the Father of Jesus. Also, it is very, very selfless: our (unfelt?) love for God overcoming self-love. Prayer is self-surrender in faith and here, I believe, we have its purest, personal expression.

With my love,

    Ruth

XVI Prayer – taking us to the edge

Very dear Ruth,

N whom I saw recently, was keen for news of you. I had sent
her your books *Before the Living God* and *Guidelines for
Mystical Prayer*, together with a small anthology of Rahner.
She has been devouring them.

She commented that she felt your writing was really a 'bit
advanced' for her, that probably you were writing for other
religious. I told her I thought not – for two reasons.

First, it is an entirely natural, but actually unhelpful, inclination
among the laity to imagine that the heart of religion is for the
clergy/periti; that there is something presumptuous in a lay
person's longing for a deeper faith. I feel this myself and
have to put it aside. The kernel of it is likely to be a form of
evasion. God's love, like His rain, falls on clergy and laity
alike. We too have to make of it what we can.

Secondly, I said that part of your conviction and the clarity of
your thought was your insistence that we have to take our
response to Jesus to the very edge: the edge we think we can
see (there is always another beyond). Only then do we grow
out of ourselves and re-examine how we are. In teaching this,
you take no prisoners, you make no compromises. You don't
blink. You hold your ground, you don't cede it. This is, of
course, maddening and a frustration, until we spot what is

going on: you are enduring your faith – exposure – what we sense when we are near the edge. The effort (and nerve) required to put up with this, is the effort which is asked of us. Your holding to your line (the Muslims say, 'Holding fast to the rope of God') is a factor for making us realise that we have to move from where we are.

A realisation deepening in me these recent weeks – and here I can only speak for myself – is that this 'going over to the edge' is crucially a matter of giving in, rather than striving. My striving self looks for and races to the next corner to one side, not the edge which is always a little way straight ahead.

For about a year my troubled back has been making my right leg a bit stiff. I have been made to do (or pretend to do) exercises to loosen it. It dawned on my stupidity in early July that really this was just a form of tension – that I had to relax, and not force, this leg. It hurts like hell to make it relax, but things are now improving. I have put the implications of this to my prayers. Why strive to go round? Why not try to allow things to be, happen, as they are – live in acceptance? Your recent comments about the God you know being a Father who longs to be used, had a strong resonance with me here. These clickings of a door behind me, shutting the way back, are wonderful moments and I am so grateful for them. Relax is a dangerous word these days. I prefer giving in, or better, giving *away*. Then unquestionably I am taken to, or towards, a new edge. It is, paradoxically, not a movement which I can make myself – only reduce resistance to it.

With much love,

Mark

XVII The barrier of fear and letting go in trust

Dearest Mark,

Your last letter stirs me. Firstly though, there is surely no need for me to say how glad I am that you didn't let N get away with it. It almost hurts me to hear people suggesting that the life of prayer, and that for me means simply a life lived by faith, a life of commitment to Jesus Our Lord, is the exclusive right of a certain class of persons. I wonder if 'right' is the correct word. What is being said, as you yourself detect, is that only this class has the obligation and responsibility for so living, the rest are blamelessly exempt. And yet, if only they could realise the treasure they are so casually dismissing! Jesus in the gospel stories speaks so often of human blindness. It seems to me our chief characteristic.

What, however, I really want to look at is the insight dawning on you. What you struggle to express is so very hard to express because it touches on something profound and immensely important. What you say brought to mind a conversation we were having some months ago at our recreation period. We were talking about what prayer means to different people and one of the sisters remarked that no one, of themselves, could come to the breakthrough, when the nature of true prayer dawns. She recalled how, for years, she had faithfully spent time in prayer, dutifully prayed and then, one day, the reality hit her: God really is. The experience was terrifying! No longer was prayer innocuous, something she did and could handle. You will understand that I am recording as best I can and as I understood what she was searching for words to describe.

If I read you aright you are referring to a similar experience though perhaps not one of the same conscious/emotional impact and this could be due to temperament. You are perceiving what you could not perceive before even though you might have had an intellectual grasp of it and the ability to explain it theoretically. I think that what lies behind N's baulking – and she represents a multitude – as well as your own previous block, is fear. The sister spoke of terror. I see no answer to this except to look at Jesus, to hear his words uttered over and over again in the pages of the gospel: 'Fear not!' Jesus our brother knows our fear and reassures us. He assures us of our loving Father's constant longing for our total well-being and happiness, assures us that it is safe to jump, to go beyond the edge because the divine arms await us and these arms are totally reliable. We can shut our eyes and hold on, no matter what; cling to the mast in the shipwreck even though it seems to be disintegrating. 'Though heaven and earth should pass away, my word will not pass away' (Mark 13:31). And that word is a guarantee of unfailing love. A devout person can go through life shielding her/himself from God through 'prayer', but it will not be because God has not worked to smash through the protection.

All the same, not for one moment do I want to decry fidelity to 'prayer' because it does give God a chance. God reads the heart, knows the fears, the inhibitions, the things which enchain a person; looks on them with compassion and gratefully accepts from this person every movement of desire and good will. To refer back to my sister, I know her well and have known her for many years and observed her fidelity and am sure that it ensured that the breakthrough could happen when the time was ripe. The enlightenment must be assented to and lived with. It would still be possible to dive for one's old bolthole after the first impact. Do you recognise anything of yourself in what I write, or have I got it all wrong?

If I am right, then it follows that the way forward is by letting go, letting be, relaxing. The latter is a dangerous word, but not when understood. Faith is like a leap – a leaving firm ground, a letting go; but surely it is easy to grasp what an act, what a real choice this is. To sustain faith, to sustain 'passivity', calls for all we have got and that is a paradox known only by experience. Christian existence is all paradox – dying we live . . .

I think someone of your temperament, background, and training will naturally have enormous difficulty with 'passivity'. As you describe so well, you are ready to dash off to confront the biggest difficulty, the challenge round the corner, one that demands and employs the full measure of your wits, energy, enterprise, where you yourself are the manager, the activator and actor. And you realise that the greatest enterprise of all, the one grace has stirred your heart to long for, cannot be embarked on in this way, it demands a laying down of your 'life', your ego. You have to become as dependent, as helpless as a little child – a child that will take one step at a time because it is incapable of more. It does not know what is round the corner, just lives its life moment by moment in trust. 'This is impossible to man but not to God, for everything is possible to God' (Matthew 19:26). God can disarm you, can enlighten you, increase your trust so that you yourself choose to become at the root of your being, a little child. These great biblical images can slip off our tongue, can't they, but oh, the reality . . .

The images I have used earlier, of clinging on in a storm, facing an abyss and choosing to jump, suggest drama; and drama and crisis at least lend interest to our inner life. Not infrequently we find it relatively easy to cope with such. But the real hanging on, the real leaping off the edge, is likely to be devoid of all drama, can, in fact, involve living on and on with 'nothing happening', God silent and hidden. And what greater test is there of faith, of the Father's loving, caring, self-giving? To my mind, it is this that terrifies us, makes us cry out, makes us thresh around for reassurance, for something to happen. I love the story of Jesus asleep in the boat in Mark's version, especially (Mark 4:35–41). Reading it carefully, it seems to me that Jesus was as good as saying that they should have been willing to go down with him in the boat! They dare not risk that so wake him up and get him to act and, of course, he does. That's what we are trying to do, isn't it, people of little faith that we are? He himself let himself go down, drown, no longer aware of his Father's presence and care, but knowing they were there all the same and trusting absolutely. Because of Jesus, in him, we too can 'drown' in nothingness.

With my love,

   Ruth

XVIII 'Who is this that even the wind and the sea obey him?' (Mark 4:41)

Very dear Ruth,

You asked in your letter whether the account you gave of what your sister had said, made sense to me.

I think that this dimension of prayer is about release, being released particularly from ambiguity. The driver of this ambiguity could well be fear. The striving self is searching. You put it right: activator and actor – I know what to do next, be active, be busy. But the search is for something which remains hidden in the ambiguity of the self's own desires: a bit for Him and, even if unconsciously, a bit for me. In this unresolved state, there is of course the frustration of not being able to see what is sought, but there is also an apparent security. I am not yet committed. I am still in charge. And the latent fact is that I am avoiding something. Yes, that avoidance is probably motivated by fear.

The release from all this – I spoke of an edge to which I turn, or rather am turned and am taken – effects at this deep level of the heart a giving away of balance, and choice. The release confronts me with a new reality. We don't want to play with words here, but I would catch something of it by saying that the heart is all set on transcendence, trying to take off from where it is; the reality is right up in front and inside,

immanent. It's as though one has been missing the point,
looking the wrong way.

The contrast between this solid reality which releases,
confronts and converts, and those shifting compounds of
ambiguous desire, is indeed striking. Terrifying? To a
sensitive and pure heart realising such a contrast might well
be terrifying. I can imagine that, though that is not what I
knew.

You write of Jesus asleep in the boat: that scene which ends
with the staggering drama of Jesus stilling the waves. And the
disciples *are* staggered: 'Who can this be that even the wind
and the sea obey him?' Perhaps they had little faith when they
had to wake Jesus up. Well, how did his demonstration of his
divine powers strike them? They have nothing to say, just a big
question to ask: 'Who is this?' And the question is *not*
answered. So God's revealing His reality does not resolve the
problem of faith. There is always another edge. The reality, the
burning bush, cannot be comprehended: it is holy Mystery.

For me that is being at the edge: enduring the absence of an
answer. Yet somehow there is a conviction that all will be well.
The waves are stilled. And doesn't Rahner mean the same
thing when he says, 'Grace does not imply the promise and the
beginning of the elimination of the mystery, but the radical
possibility of the absolute proximity of the mystery, which
is not eliminated by its proximity, but really presented as
mystery'?

Faith emerges from this as a dimension of continuing
conversion. It is not an address which we can reach. It cannot
be opened to show its contents. It does, however, make its
conversions which seem to be from subject to object, from
meriting to gratuitously receiving. In this dimension, the heart

may find it has less to say for itself. It is not distracted by the reflexive working of the mind. It is on receive, not transmit. It does not expect to register or understand what is being received. It may, or may not, realise in retrospect that something has been learned. In its now that can all be left for the future and then be about the past.

Last night, I came across something which struck me very hard. St John Chrysostom says, I read in a commentary on the Letter to the Hebrews, 'All men fear death; therefore to enable us to take death in our stride, He tasted death even though it was not necessary for Him to do so.' (*Homilies on the Letter to the Hebrews*, 4). Jesus, in his humanity, is also showing us *how* . . .

Now that I've read that, I can see further into your 'Because of Jesus, in Him, we too can "drown" in nothingness'.

What a long and roundabout way. Is this where you stopped your letter?

With much love,

Mark

XIX Responding to the Holy Spirit

Dearest Mark,

Many, many thanks for sharing with me your friend John's perceptive and useful commentary on our exchanges on prayer. I pick out the points I think most important and which I can say something about.

I quote him: 'I suspect that the heart as well as the mind should be enlisted if, as was my experience, the first stage was to be helped to feel a thirst for God like "a dry weary land without water" that drives the soul to "muse on You through the night".'

Well, we surely agree with that, don't we? But I must add a cautionary question as to what we mean by the heart and what John means by 'feel'. If I am right – I go by the testimony of his letter – his conversion experience was accompanied by deep emotion and I think this is true for many, perhaps most, but not for all and I have a concern for those who know little or no religious emotion because they need a lot of reassurance and encouragement. I do not equate the heart with feeling in the usual meaning of the term and yet do not identify it with the mind. In the context in which I am employing it now, it is, I think, the inmost self, appreciating, recognising the worth of values and responding. It is as if the inmost self has fingers with which it carefully feels all around a subject and declares it good, desirable. The mind is, of course, playing a part but – and it is here I agree with John – there has to be this inner 'feeling' for there to be conviction and choice.

It seems to me that all genuine spirituality is an interplay of the personal existential experience and objective reality. For us, the supreme objective reality is divine revelation which gives meaning to everything. The miracle of conversion is born of this interplay, is it not? Not infrequently it will be by hearing the creative 'word' from without: in a sermon, conversation, book. An inner chord is struck and the hearer looks into her or his heart, into its actual experience which perhaps, up to this point, has been unconsciously or may be quite consciously avoided. For another it will be the other way round: some deep experience, probably of sorrow and loss; the crumbling of the familiar, seemingly secure world; the invasion of fear; the sense of emptiness and of life being meaningless. And let us not forget the experience of great love or the breaking in of unexpected joy. The heart longing for meaning, for value looks 'outside'. Inner lack prompts search 'without'. The transcendent experiences of love and joy are pointing beyond themselves to the Absolute. In all cases there is a choice. Values have been recognised or at least glimpsed, but will they be embraced, acted upon, conformed to and thus lead to further insight?

We cannot know how often this precious showing, this 'dawning' is ignored, forgotten and night is chosen. There is an unbridgeable gap between seeing/hearing a creative, life-giving 'word' (that can come as event, an inner or outward experience) and its fruit-bearing. The gospels bear ample witness to this phenomenon, the gospel of John in particular. 'Men chose darkness rather than light' (John 3:19), is his tragic lament: they saw him, heard him, touched him, observed his way of being, his 'good works' and yet did not see, did not hear. It would seem that for others, insight dawned, but

*they turned away from it as too disturbing and eventually in
their fear, got rid of the One who embodied light, the light that
is the life, true life of humankind. But there were those who
welcomed the light and these could exclaim rapturously: 'We
ourselves have seen, heard, touched the very Word who is life'.
Ultimately it is the Holy Spirit who bridges the unbridgeable
gap between belief and unbelief. 'The love of God has been
poured into our hearts by the Holy Spirit who has been given
to us.' We have to accept, make room, do all that is in our
power to cooperate.*

*John would have liked me to supply meditations on the love of
God that would stir and warm the heart. I think it is more
important to urge people to seek, in their own circumstances
and according to their own personality, for this food. It has to
be sought. Initially it may seem to drop like manna from
heaven, but that won't continue. Eventually we have to dig and
cultivate the land to obtain our food. We can't overestimate the
advantage of having friends who are perhaps a little more
experienced than ourselves, who will inspire us, share with us
their own understanding. I could write sheaves of meditations
on the gospels but there would be no guarantee that those who
read them would find them helpful. We differ so much in our
personalities, background, education and so forth. Always we
are thrown back on personal choice and responsibility. No one
can choose for us, no one can do the work for us. Grace is
offered, is all around us but we must use it.*

*I have been struck by the gospel readings at Mass in these last
weeks of Lent. All that interest and talk about Jesus: 'What do
you think about him?' 'Will he come up for the feast?' 'He is a
good man.' 'How can he be?' 'Is his the Messiah?' 'Have the
authorities decided he is the Messiah?' 'He can't be the
Messiah because . . .' Discussion, seemingly genuine interest
in Jesus; a waiting for 'authority' to make the decision for*

them – what looks like honest searching is mere evasion of the responsibility of having to make a choice and act on it. And this leads me to John's stricture that I am unhelpfully hard on the lady you mention (cf. letter XI). 'I am reminded', he writes, 'of what a priest friend once told me, that he hardly ever accused penitents of lack of seriousness, or impenitence, even if they obviously needed help towards reconciliation: if they were not serious or penitent, why should they be kneeling in that dark stuffy box in order to participate in that wonderful but far from easy sacrament?' Why indeed?! This penitent has done something and probably at great cost and there he is on his knees! But our 'instance', what is she doing? On her own admission, nothing. The penitent said, 'I want to go to confession,' and he got up and went. Our 'instance' says: 'I would like to pray,' and does nothing, save say so! But let me repeat what I said in that particular letter, that this 'friend' was, for me, merely an instance that, were I in contact with a living person, no doubt I would take a different approach. But I wanted to stress the need for choice, for real action, not just wishful thinking that gets us nowhere.

There are one or two more points to look at, Mark, but I would rather conclude this letter now and get it off.

With my love,

    Ruth

XX Conversion and conviction

Very dear Ruth,

Heart, conversion, choice and action.

Heart. Where is all this going on? You slip a scalpel under the soft tissue of feelings and separate that from what you mean by the heart and you go on to speak of the 'innermost self'. In your first letter you wrote, ' . . . we have to reflect more deeply and admit to a dimension of ourselves that, though it expresses itself through ordinary, conscious experience yet is, I think we may say, independent of it. It is this dimension which will develop in prayer . . . Of its very nature – it is where the divine, Holy Spirit "dwells", communes – it cannot be available to our ordinary consciousness any more than can the holy One whose "dwelling" it is'.

The place in ourselves where the Holy Spirit may work in us, is ultimately secret. I like the old-fashioned 'soul' – it is still a good word. We can accept the soul's existence, not just as the 'real me', but as the immortal dimension of whatever it is that is me. We are taught that from the very beginning. It's not so difficult to differentiate this from 'mind'. But to say that there are things going on in the soul which are not apparent or only to be recognised in retrospect – that's harder. We do find it much more difficult to accept the secrecy of the soul. But that's a vital thing to take on trust. How else, where else, may real contact between the Holy Spirit and the self be taking place? Or are we actually still secretly doubting that it may be – unless we can monitor it? Don't we have to remind ourselves that growth in the life of the spirit cannot be watched 'in real time', contemporaneously, any more than can our physical growth when we are young. We need somehow to accept that our attempts to get our own access into the soul and have a good look round, just don't work. We are looking then into mirrors.

You speak of the 'miracle of conversion' and 'an unbridgeable gap' which can only be the province of the Holy Spirit and at first this seems rather stark, rather discouraging. I think there is an issue of encouragement and reassurance – you mention those who 'know little or no religious emotion' – but doesn't it crop up much later on, something for a later letter: the self's difficulty in trusting that something is going on, rather than can go on? We may not dare God to speak a little louder, a little more gently, or however we may need, in our own temperamental moment. I think it is safer, if one can, to opt to do without encouragement. It won't last; we are always on the look out for reassurance from others at the emotional level which seems to count; but the option to do without may make us more alive to how separate this level of feeling truly is from the soul, and turn the eye outwards from our natural need to be the centre of our own concerns. That may sound hard. But isn't that the startling immediacy of the vocation addressed to us, to allow now the limits of what we think we can manage to be tested? How else do we learn to walk, learn to love?

I feel a bit cagey about conversion. If conversion is very nearly the same as prayer which may be either a moment of sentient transcendence apprehended as prayerful, or a long struggle, then, like prayer, conversion takes a lifetime. It is an unending intention towards the kingdom which is beyond and outside time. Conversion then is not something we can say 'has happened', save in the limited sense of confessional assent. The 'born again' language which is rooted properly in baptism, runs that risk of suggesting that there is an event which one might look back on. A corner turned perhaps, but it's hard to see an end to prayer or an end to conversion.

You put the accent on choice and action, doing something which will support the act of will to be open to God. What you wrote puts me in mind of Adam being told, 'By the sweat of your face will you earn your food' (Genesis 3:19). We are faced with the ghastly paradox that we must work at faith, at prayer, at love, yet all for a God who is omnipotently striving to reach us with his love. 'The religious life is full of paradox', you wrote. Learning to accept the paradoxes seems to me to be the main business of life, the anvil of prayer on which we hammer out our readiness to say a sincere 'Yes', an 'Amen' to the immeasurable encouragement and support which is there in that objective reality. No matter how dark, how blinding its inaccessible light, we have to hold to the conviction that it is Love, explained to us by and in the person of Christ.

I think there is a metaphor of all this in marriage. You say you agree with John that there has to be 'this inner feeling' for there to be conviction and choice. The young couples to bet on are those who speak of not being able to look ahead at life, one without the other. There is conviction. The choice is almost made. Conviction comes from the Latin root meaning to conquer. The young couple are literally conquered by their love. The choices which follow to marry and those made in marriage, are rational, if motivated from within. As life goes on, fidelity to these choices and the self-discipline in making them together frame and define the whole person to depths understood at the outset but learned in quite a new way once they have been searched and explored. And we can't see it happening. We see that it has happened. And isn't prayer like that?

With much love,

Mark

XXI Immortality and our choice

Dearest Mark,

Who can explain precisely what we mean by 'heart' and yet, don't we all, instinctively, know? I avoid the very useful word 'soul' because it implies duality, that we are compounded of body and that, whereas the body is mortal, the soul is immortal. This leads us to the reassuring (?) conclusion that there is an inalienable element in us that is of itself immortal. I cannot think that this is true. The way I think about it is this. We are animals that can think and can choose. The fact that we can think opens us to the infinite horizon of mystery. I believe that 'from the outset' – the scriptural 'in the beginning' (meaning it never was not so), human beings, these thinking animals are graced, in relation to God . . . made for Yourself and ever desiring, restless, seeking their absolute Love. The Light enlightens every mortal being 'from the outset'. I think I would call that inmost desiring, yearning, the 'heart'. It is the effect of grace, of God's will to draw us into His own life. It is rooted in the ability to choose, in our freedom to choose.

Human beings desire happiness and are endlessly seeking for it. They are longing for what is beautiful, good and, ultimately, for what is absolutely so. In the measure that we choose rightly, choose what is really true and good, we become ever more authentically human and our Maker and Lover is able to communicate with us in increasing fullness. We become imbued with eternal life, God's own life. Immortality is a pure gift. It does not belong to our nature of itself. But our Creator and Lover wants us and wants us 'forever' with him; will never let us go, be snuffed out, let us vanish like the grass of the field, because He loves us. We have no other guarantee of life everlasting in whatever form, except God's faithful love.

Is this a needless digression? Possibly. But it led naturally from my thinking of heart. Let's say 'heart' is myself choosing; let's say it is myself-in-God's-heart and always moved by God to want Him and to seek Him. We can't take a peek inside and see that self-in-God. And maybe this sense of unknowing, of obscurity regarding that inmost self, grows as we grow. I agree that we must accept to be secret from ourselves.

I used the word 'conversion' in a conventional way denoting that 'moment' – not infrequently it is a memorable event – when a person, hitherto rather heedless of divine things, casual in relation to life's deepest meaning, is suddenly enlightened, shocked into realisation and, of course, is faced with the decision to live a 'Yes' or a 'No' (I think a luke-warm 'Yes' is really a 'No'). From John's testimony, his 'conversion' had something of this. There are plenty of instances in Scripture: Paul's conversion is classic. However, I do agree that its use in such a particular context can be dangerous. We are always being converted, always challenged to turn away from selfishness, from whatever is not God, to God. What is more, there are plenty of true disciples who have never experienced anything dramatic in their lives, their understanding and love quietly developing over their years. On the other hand, a devout person of proven fidelity can undergo a shattering experience of conversion – or rather is offered such a grace when she or he sees the shallowness, the basic self-orientation in what they had hitherto presumed to be their devotion to God. The 'experience' remains, as you suggest, not conversion in itself, but the offer of the grace of conversion, to be accepted, and laboured over to bring to realisation.

I love your last paragraph. Oh, how mysterious we are! 'Who has known the mind of the Lord?' (Romans 11:34). I think we can equally exclaim, 'Who has known the human mind?' (or should we say 'heart'?). Where does it come from, that conviction? Why does this person 'know' and another does not? The heart has its own mysterious reasons. I think we have to leave it at that. Human freedom is a marvellous gift that is a huge responsibility. It rests with us to say, 'Yes' to God, or to say, 'No'. I can understand Thérèse of Lisieux's cry that God would take away her will for fear it should say, 'No' even in apparently small matters. How we must trust Him, lean upon Him and not at all upon ourselves! I am beginning to get lost and to waffle so I must stop. I doubt if I have answered you in any real way.

With my love,

Ruth

XXII Accepting purification

Dearest Mark,

John admits to a 'lingering unease' with my assertion that 'prayer is essentially what God does in us, not what we do'. He would like to substitute something like, 'depends ultimately on'. 'Otherwise', he writes, 'much of the biblical teaching . . . concerned as it is primarily with our contribution to the process of prayer, would be side-lined as irrelevant to the essence of prayer, which it patently is not.' I have no difficulty with this modification but John's unease means that I must spell out more carefully what I mean by my own statement which I believe to be expressing a vitally important truth.

I doubt if anyone committed to prayer would have any difficulty in affirming John's statement – in theory. But my long experience has shown me times without number that, in practice, it is not so. There is no question of my suggesting that we have no part to play in prayer, no work to do. A little earlier I spoke of digging for our food: reading, reflecting, consulting and, of course, living our days in the light of faith which involves asceticism, discipline – we can say truly that prayer is a full-time job! Then there is the immediate preparation: gathering ourselves up as best we can, going apart if possible. Is it always possible for a family man or woman, living in a small house, to withdraw to an inner room physically speaking? Each one of us has to plan intelligently.

But I do think that within the actual time-space we give to prayer, then we should sit loose in the saddle and drop the reins, or hold them slack. Now it is God's turn. Our 'work' is to believe and, as far as we can, maintain the faith-attitude: 'I know I am in Your loving presence. Please work in me as You want. Give me Yourself which is what You want to do . . .' We will have to keep fuelling that faith, redirecting ourselves if we have wandered off; reaffirm our belief if we get discouraged and so forth, and so forth. It is a sort of non-passive passivity, a quiet reaching out, a longing and, of course, a self-surrender. In effect we are saying: 'Here I am helpless. You must do everything for me' and that is simple unassailable truth. We cannot rise to God, raise ourselves upwards. God comes to us and lifts us up.

Now to my contention that, in practice, we do not believe. If we look closely we might find that our preparation for prayer, our work at prayer, 'our side' of the process of prayer is permeated with the desire for 'success'. At bottom we are wanting 'to pray' and to know we pray and pray well. Our desire can be more for 'prayer' than for God. We want successful prayer, we want manifest returns and we are prepared to invest a lot of effort into all this. I am far, far from saying that it is all ego. Not at all. I am only highlighting our inevitable, inescapable, often unconscious self-seeking, even in prayer. Only God can get us to see this and purify us of it and this He will do if we allow it. And when this happens in earnest we shall have a choice: Do I really believe that 'prayer is essentially what God does in us and not what we do', or not?

If we choose the first then we shall persevere through thick and thin, never getting discouraged, never giving up even through long years of 'barrenness' with 'nothing happening', with no returns. If we insist on controlling our prayer, making it work, when God is wanting to wean us away from our being so busy, what we think of as our prayer is no longer prayer but a subtle form of spiritual pride. Once we really understand and really believe, such laments as: 'I can't pray today, I am as dry as sticks'; 'I can't get in touch with God, so I'll do something useful instead'; 'I'm too tired to pray'; 'I just can't pray and that's that!' are nonsense.

Of course John is right in emphasising our part. The choice to pray, the dogged perseverance which can be so very costly, the 'labour' are essential. We have Jesus' own words that we must go on praying and never give up though seemingly ignored. I find this such a moving story, the importunate widow and the unjust judge (Luke 18:1–8). Jesus knew that his loving Father can seem 'unjust', obdurate, indifferent to us and gives us no reward for our devotion. 'Don't take any notice of what it seems like, I know the reality,' is what he is saying; 'just go on: ask and you will receive, seek and you will find, knock and the door will be opened.' Do we really believe this? We must put all the weight on Jesus' words and end our worries and concern as to whether we have got it right. Am I praying? Am I using the right knocker or is there another one I haven't seen? We can be far more occupied with the way we are knocking and asking than with the heart of God.

Mark, I don't think John has understood what I mean by poverty when I say it is humanly repulsive. I can't take back what I say. Maybe what I have just hinted at regarding the way God weans us from our self-seeking, supports my meaning. Why do people give up prayer when the first fervour has past? Why do those who persevere thresh around so much wanting to be shown, to be reassured, to feel they are successful? All these anxieties reveal a dread of feeling a spiritual failure, helpless, sinful . . . totally poor. There is no point in spelling it out. Words are mere words. I do, however, agree that we can come to love this naturally repulsive poverty but only in the light of faith and love, only contemplation of Jesus the Beloved. St Thérèse of the Infant Jesus has taught us so much about all this and could roundly declare that God's greatest gift to her and that which pleased God most in her, was the experience of, and loving acceptance of, her poverty. But make no mistake about it, she was speaking of what was naturally a painful experience. The humiliated, bruised, despised face of Jesus in his passion was her paradigm and that must give us thought.

As we grow in love – or so I understand – what we ourselves are like, what we are, feel about ourselves or how we stand spiritually – means less and less and eventually not at all. I think it must be something of what Paul means in speaking of the loss of everything, counting all as naught so as to have nothing but Christ, sharing in his death so as to share his resurrection. Naturally, we want to live our own life – of course we do – and we want God somehow to infuse it with divine glory and so enhance our life, making our life divine. That can't be. We must live by Jesus' life, eternal life, God's life, and this means losing our own. 'Dying' to our own life is, humanly speaking, not nice! And maybe the deepest meaning of Jesus' injunction to avoid all 'show' in our praying, to enter our secret chamber and with the door firmly shut, pray to 'your Father in secret', is this self-forgetfulness, this self-loss which ensures total exposure to the Father which is pure prayer.

With my love,

    Ruth

XXIII Reassurance and communication

Very dear Ruth,

Your second letter arrived before you will have got my last
one. I shall make sure John gets copies of yours. He will be
delighted. You deal unambiguously with his 'lingering unease'.
The final scenes in the main street in that stunning film, 'High
Noon', come to mind, but I don't suppose you've seen it. Or
have you?

I am not going to try to comment on what you wrote because it
was so clear and to the point. I have put it by for re-reading.

I want to put to you something you touched on in your previous
letter and which I thought might have to wait a while, but
now will do. I set it now against the light of your last letter,
especially your passage on poverty.

What is to be said about encouragement and reassurance? You
said that those with little or no religious emotion needed it. I
said that in the early stages when one is having to make early
choices and rearrange things, as you wrote 'plan intelligently',
it's a wise counsel to try to do without encouragement. You
can say if you think this is too harsh. I think that for some,
certainly for me, having to suffer the lip-biting absence of any
'success' in prayer is a good way of having to face up to the
nasty fact that my worry is all about me, not about God. The
Father is himself, revealed to us in His Son, present to us in

the Spirit. The mind doesn't find a way round that. So where's the worry? It is, as you say, inside the self, for the self. I think that if I had had some director or guide encouraging me, I might well have missed the necessary deductions.

Time passes. I accept with my mind the theology of the Spirit praying in me (Romans 8:26–7). I don't blink at distractions. Sometimes I don't even make much effort to gather them up and put them on one side. Distractions? Well, they would, wouldn't they? Occasionally, apparently prayerful and helpful thoughts come up. You know that old one about the silence (that is, the noise of the world) being the sound of God himself? All this. I don't mind or pause about it. Then, one day, I do notice that all this seems extremely insignificant and I wonder whether I could even truthfully say, if interrupted, that I am trying to pray. I could only say that it would be open to me to do something else with the time, but I am not. It comes to my understanding that this is exactly what prayer can be an absolute secret. Since then I have had less trouble.

I mention this so that you can tell me you never meant the reins to be quite that slack, or so that you can say whether you agree that we do ourselves no service by wanting to be in on the secret. If you do agree, then there is a sort of encouragement. It's a paradox, but if we have made an honest effort to place ourselves in front of the Lord and can then leave the action to him, then the mind and personality, our very active bits, can stand down for a while. A time comes when it is not a great matter to get them to stand down, it just isn't an issue because prayer does not depend on whether that has been 'achieved' or not.

Implicit in this, and I hasten to add that I am not now existing in a complete fog of disconnection, is a question of what to make of 'communication'. I am not speaking of what are

technically called 'locutions', voices and sentences heard
in the soul (or the ears!), but of what seems more like
commonsense rising to the surface, different to, but not
unlike, the voice of conscience.

People often say, when in some difficulty, 'Well, I have prayed
a lot about this and have to say that . . . ' and some definite
position follows, and sometimes quite a polemical one. Hardly
for me to comment on their own dialogue in prayer, but I can
say that these are dialogues which have not occurred to me. I
have never had any practical advice. Indeed, and for me this is
a heavy paradox, I have met with a support which I cannot
explain, by relying on the thought that outside His revelation,
nothing which I might identify with God actually is God. He is
always further on.

If it is the Holy Spirit who prays 'according to the mind of
God' (ibid), then can we say God may reveal something about
himself in this discourse? This is unlikely to be startling. Has
He not revealed himself already? But He may reinforce, in a
way which is sensible only in retrospect, a conviction which
does want to grow and which therefore eases the chafing of the
choices which that small conviction feels it has to make. That
is not the same as identifying for one the particular choices to
be made.

The principal arena of choice is 'dying' to the world and what
this means for me. Our deaths are individual, even if outwardly
the same. All that you wrote about this made me think of
Adam again and that fearsome first temptation, 'You shall be
as Gods' (Genesis 3:5) which they bought into. I find that
almost casual succumbing to that temptation a much more
telling illumination of Original Sin than the burden of guilt
which we bring from childhood about pinching sweets and
being horrid to others. And even for a follower of Jesus,

poverty can be the next crown. I could not agree with you
more. Poverty elevated to some recherché meaning just ain't
poor. It looks pretty smug. Living quietly the bitterness in
interior 'dying' is quite another matter from embracing poverty
as an assurance of being on the right track. I just don't believe
it's possible without a large conviction that faith in the end,
and now, is worth the risk, that the life of Jesus is a better life
than my own life. In the end, if given its chance, I think faith
takes the place of encouragement.

With much love,

    Mark

XXIV Consolations and where God reveals His will

Dearest Mark,

You leave me wondering what on earth there is to say. Your letter is its own answer, carries an authority which needs no authentication from me. However, there are two or three comments I would make, for I know you want me to say something and would feel I had given you short shrift if I limited myself to that opening sentence. Also, I'm a Carmelite and eschew the indiscriminate use of funds and so will get my money's worth from even a second-class stamp by enclosing, with her permission, another letter which I had recently from one of my Sisters, together with my reply. So many of the problems which people seem to have with prayer are also about the mind and what to do with it. She looks at this and I hope our exchange may be of help to you.

It has been your experience, Mark, that to lack the assurance and encouragement that another person might have given you, proved to be a blessing. But we mustn't generalise. You are singularly equipped and not everyone is as gifted as you. I see the way of prayer as unique to each individual and believe that God guides each one with finesse. There is nothing about this guidance that 'shouts aloud in the street', that goes around placarding itself as 'Divine Guidance'. No, it is concealed within the workings of our own mind,

*entangled in the strands of our temperament, present in all
the persons and events life brings to us. I believe that, if we
really seek God, we do obtain all we need, 'Give us this day
our daily bread'. If God sees we need assurance, He will
ensure that the right person, or the right book, comes along
at the right moment.*

*Yet always our freedom is respected. Always we have the
choice of seeing, or not seeing, hearing, or not hearing,
accepting or rejecting. As you make clear, you have been
inspired, guided to see, hear the word of God and to believe
and make that your certainty, regardless of your confusions
and the 'labyrinthine ways' of your own mind. Not all, at
least to begin with, find such ready access to Scripture and
they need to be 'built up' by a believer's word. Not all have
the ability or the opportunity to study the books you have
studied and may well find themselves bewildered to begin
with. I agree that, once we have really gazed into the face of
Christ, we find our answer and can let go, but most people, if
not all, need help to reach that point.*

*When I have been writing about prayer, I have made a point of
addressing myself to those who experience little or no religious
emotion in order to encourage them. I do this because it would
seem that spiritual writers tend to take it for granted that,
sooner or later, consolation will come, and that we must
indeed persevere in difficulties which are sure to be there, but
looking forward to the day when the sun will shine. Almost
always the implication, even though very subtle, is that
consolation is the real thing, real prayer. The writer might
deny this and yet, it seems to me, that as often as not the
implication is there. This, I believe, has to be firmly refuted.
In no way is it decrying the reality of consolation and its
desirability, but it may not be identified with prayer itself. It
may accompany prayer, but prayer is equally real without it.*

*As I was re-reading this letter so far, the thought was
emerging that really Mark has been just as dependent on
'outside' assurance and encouragement as anyone else. We
simply cannot do without the Christian community. We need
each other to enlighten and support each other. All he has got
has come through the community. After all, the Scriptures and
especially the New Testament emerge from the community and
ultimately, it's the same thing whether one finds all the
support one needs there or whether the Lord sends a
contemporary as His angel to bear His good news, His
message of love and care to us.*

*You don't, of course, need my assurance! But I'll give it all
the same. I share your scepticism regarding 'communications'
in prayer. Nothing is easier or more open to deception than to
claim, 'I have prayed about this' and therefore the conclusion
I have drawn must be right. I for one have too much
self-doubt, am too aware of how I can get the answer I want
to get! Most certainly we must pray, but for purity of heart,
for the firm resolve to give God all God asks. We must pray to
do God's will and not our own, do what is truly good not
what we want to think is good. Then, it's a case of using our
minds as responsibly, as authentically as we can, asking
advice, looking all round the subject, facing up to our own
fears, desires, prejudices and struggling to leave them aside
as we examine the question and make our decision. Oh, there
is no nice, pious, short cut! It's part and parcel of God's
finesse in guidance, concealed in our own processes, in the
proper use of the faculties He has given us and allowing us
the glory of freedom to choose Him or to reject Him. Yes, that
is the stark reality behind our half-chosen blindness, our
cowardice and subtle self-seeking cloaked in piety.*

*Spiritual poverty, Mark, I won't touch again. It's too easily
taintable.*

*Well, I haven't done badly, have I? But here I do take my
leave.*

With my love,

   Ruth

   Dear Ruth,

   This won't be news to you for you have heard me talk about it in one
   way or another many times. It is the relationship between prayer and
   thought. From my background I absorbed the conviction that thought
   was the highest human activity. Although I recognise that my family
   may have been unusually intellectual, I think I share this lot with
   liberal English culture. Even though my family was loving, love was
   not taught explicitly as a value on a par with thought. I think without
   exaggerating, that I am a child of the Enlightenment in this. It was
   after many years of struggle and relatively late that I came to the
   realisation that prayer is a higher activity than thought. And that had
   been my block.

   When I told you of this breakthrough, you replied by saying that
   prayer is not an activity. Perhaps you were right. I am not sure that I
   want to get sidetracked on that problem now. What I simply mean is
   that it was a breakthrough for me to see that, as a way of spending
   time, there is for a human being nothing higher than prayer, and this,
   of course, includes liturgical prayer. Obviously when that is in place
   all activities gain in value, as prayer does not compete in that sense.
   But I can think of no better way of saying it – we are most human
   when we are praying. And so if movement forward in prayer demands,
   for example, sacrificing clarity of thought, that sacrifice has to be
   made. It may be very hard for you, a Christian and a Catholic from
   your birth, to understand what a breakthrough this was for me, and
   how it made it easier for me happily to overcome resistances in
   myself.

   Part of the problem is, I think, that prayer is not often experienced as
   a 'high' activity. It brings us face to face with our lowliness. So that
   every value judgement is an act of faith. But there is something else
   operating. Prayer does change reality – gradually re-orientates us

with respect to all reality – ourselves, other people, God and creation. Thought depends on some predictable structure of reality which can be explored. I wonder if that is not why thought, in any kind of clinging sense, in any desire to erect its own structures, has to go. I wonder too if that is not my answer to the question of the place of the mind in Carmel. We are to live at the most radical turning point of prayer for the world – mirrored for us in the Cross. It is a point of deep change, but one which thought cannot penetrate. Our own thought has to become servant. But as it points us to the next step, it may constantly have to let go of vision, over and over again. It is more important that we love, that we 'die', that reality be changed, than that we understand. But I don't see this process as arbitrary. So, as I said, it is served by thought. I'm not sure if I have answered my own question, but would like to hear what your comments are.

With love and thanks,

    Emily

    My dear Emily,

You answer your own question, don't you? And that is always the best way. What follows is only verifying what you say. I can't remember the occasion you refer to, when I said that prayer was not an activity but I can well imagine myself saying it to you! There you would be stressing and straining to grasp, to somehow make sense of God, to have clear ideas as to what you were supposed to be doing in prayer, trying to get hold of God with your mind, earnest, longing ... And I would come in and say, 'But prayer isn't an activity, not something you do; it's what God does.' You see it now, in your own way.

To say that prayer is not an activity in itself is inaccurate for of course it is. It would not be human, if it were not. Prayer is something that we do: we choose it, set aside time, summon attention as best we can. My emphasis was on prayer as response, a response of faith to the divine Mystery of Love always offering Itself, drawing us into Its enfolding, transforming Self. It is a choosing to allow God to act, to saying with our whole being, often in intellectual darkness and emotional barrenness, 'Fiat'. This is human activity and, as you so rightly say, the highest form.

To take up your idea of thought as the servant of faith and love: Yes, indeed, and an industrious servant at that, but not during the time set aside for prayer. At prayer time, we need to be as free and unencumbered as birds, letting the currents take us. If we are drawn to reflection, then we follow that drawing, but we do not set out to do, think, struggle to hold our own. In prayer time, the initiative must be handed over in faith and blind trust to the Holy Spirit. We must not control our prayer.

Outside the time of prayer, however, according to our intellectual capacity and opportunity, we have the duty to apply our minds to the forms, facts, words, structures of divine revelation. This means, of course, getting to know Jesus – but always aware that the content can never be grasped by the human mind; the content is pure gift to us, infused into our inmost heart. We may not be aware that we have received this reality but we must never doubt that, if we seek with reverent, utterly humble faith, we 'find'. Our study must be pervaded throughout by the implicit and often explicit 'Lord, that I may see! Show me what you mean in the way and in the measure that you want me to understand.' At the end of it all we may feel barren and unenlightened. Humility and trust accept this. If we were concerned with a secular subject we would just go on trying to crack the nut, but not so in theology. Here we are dealing with what is essentially holy Mystery – the revelation of Absolute Love in Christ which surpasses all understanding and always will.

Nevertheless, although our minds can never encompass this holy Mystery, through Its divine working, our surrender to It can be total and that is what matters. That is love, human love transformed in the Holy Spirit to become in very truth Jesus' own totally adequate return of love to Love. This is the real meaning of prayer. We shall never fully grasp what it means to have been given Jesus who alone can take us to the Father, into the depths of the holy Mystery. What matters is to trust, to be abandoned and allow ourselves to be divested of our own will, our pretensions, self-protectiveness and self-importance. 'Lord, that we may see!' (Mark 15:32).

With my love,

Ruth

XXV Consolations, hearing the Word and the demands of love

Very dear Ruth,

Your last letter reached me in these remote hills, wild now with cloud and rain. I don't really feel like walking and there's a cold breeze which seems to be coming out of Russia. So it has been good to have your letter to reflect on by a June fireside. Thank you for the company of it and thank you for letting me see the letter from your Sister and your reply. Yes, it seems to me she did answer her own question and very acutely too.

I have had to re-write my reply to your letter and am starting again. You said something very important about consolations and I hope you will develop that. Here I am going to try to set out what I find are the difficult edges. It may give you something against which to draw out your thoughts.

'Gazing into the face of Christ, we know . . . ' You wrote this in answer to questions I was asking about 'communications'. Your answers helped me to see that faith asks us not to dwell on any impression or experience and take it as being of the Father. What occurs to us is not God. We have to let these things go. What we have is the Word, the enduring gift which the Father has sent. The Word, however, itself tells only of the Father as beyond and yet present, having spoken and yet resounding.

We have to be able to admit, don't we, that we can have heard the Word? How? Here what you say about the heart is convincing. In our living, we realise that the Word is at work in us, is being heard and even listened to in us, and if not by me, then certainly by another. And this is apparent to us because, as the years pass, we know new depths, we see new things in once familiar sights. We can affirm that we are touched by the Word and also that we are indirectly deepened by experience. This for me is why silent, unoccupied prayer is a way that must be walked: it is placing our capacity to be touched and to experience at the disposal intentionally of God. And the heart of this is that because we usually experience nothing in prayer, we are brought starkly before that imperative of faith – not to settle down, but to look ahead without, as you said to Emily, any sensible hope at the time of being able to see anything. This unoccupied prayer leaves the self open and exposed not only to the secret work of God, but also to some experience of itself. And this experience is purifying. Prayer, as time goes by, cannot but leave us a little humbler, a little more persuaded that we have to act to change, have to surrender to that call of love, have to trust to faith: all that you write about choice. In this, I see what is meant by the, at first baffling, idea which Emily voiced that prayer is the best thing, the most important thing we can do.

'Gaze into the face of Christ . . . ' I could never say that I have done that. My literal mind can't make sense of it. And my heart? I can say that I can only understand what takes place in my life, looking back over it and holding on to the objective reality of the Word, as being an exposure to the action, yes, of a person. That person, in faith, I take to be Christ: ever secretly present, ever consistent and consonant with his unceasing revelation of himself in the Word.

That this action in the world is a person, I saw particularly

through the optic of that astonishing book *God For Us* by your
late friend, Catherine Mowry LaCugna. She examines the idea
that personhood in Jesus, and therefore also in us, is 'ecstasis
of nature' – the giving out of itself, the giving away of the self.
Our experience of others and ourselves is of a personhood
which reveals and utters our flawed natures; whereas the
person of Christ, the Word, resonates the perfection of the
Father's will which is Love. In his living for his Father's will,
Jesus gives away that inexhaustible goodness. His action of
living for others makes his life an ecstasis of his nature which
is received from the Father and is absolute goodness. LaCugna
quotes from St Augustine, 'Because God is good, we exist.'
We are called to personhood: to be, to give away, to pass on
what we are given, in sacrifice of love.

The heart, empowered by faith, can sense but cannot
comprehend that goodness. The passing experience of life
reveals it as better yet than we could have believed before, and
so on. But if this is consolation, the mystery of the sacrifice of
the cross tells also of a goodness and love which cannot rest,
but must go on, beyond what was conceivable before. The
realisation that in this there is truly a person at work dawns
with the sense that none of this is our doing. All is done for us
and through the sacramental life of the Church as we receive
from others: persons enacting the goodness we receive through
Christ, the Person who in the Spirit is at work in the goodness
of people. Jesus himself tells us the truth about goodness,
'Why do you call me good? No one is good but God alone'
(Mark 10:18).

So the idea that there is a Person active in sustaining each
of our lives, which might at first appear to be consoling – a
comfortable arrangement of the dismaying muddle of life – is
not so at all. This is a Person of a different order whom
we may understand only by surrendering to a call that we

ourselves become persons in a new sense from what we ordinarily understand. On the staircase of this journey, my banister, like a piece of rock, has one word running through it: Hope. Hope does help. There's no doubt about it. Can you draw out a distinction between hope and consolation?

How do these thoughts track what was in your mind when you wrote of 'gazing into the face of Christ'?

With much love

    Mark

Dearest Mark,

Thank you for your letter. I sympathise with you having had to sit by a fire in so-called flaming June with that glorious, rolling countryside outside your windows, curtained with cloud and rain. 'It's an ill wind . . . ', however, and it gave you opportunity for reflection. Your normal lifestyle is very pressured. I myself have time for reflection as I go about my household jobs, but not so much time for getting down to writing letters. However, here goes.

'Gazing into the face of Christ' means, I believe, the same as listening to the Word. It's an echo of Paul's 'light of the knowledge of the glory of God in the face of Christ' (2 Corinthians 4:6). As I understand it – and I am sure I have said it all before – it's, so to speak, a double process: we do what we can to learn about Christ Jesus, that is, use our ordinary faculties to learn what we can of him and his vision of God and created reality, trying at the same time, to conform our minds and our actions to him. This loving effort opens us to the hidden action of God within and through this hidden action we are gradually transformed into his likeness. We gaze 'outwardly' with our normal faculties and, through divine gift, are shown 'inwardly'. I understand it as sacramental in nature.

We hear the Word, really choose to listen to it which means

*affirming it and trying to live by it, and then its content, the
Word, is received. I think most of Chapter 6 of the gospel of
John is precisely about this sacrament of the Word. 'It was
not Moses who gave you the bread from heaven; it is my
Father who gives you the bread from heaven, the true bread;
for the bread of God is the bread which comes down from
heaven and gives life to the world' (John 6:32–3). In the
scriptural sense, as well you know, 'Word' embraces works
as well as words: everything audible, visual and tangible
and supremely, Jesus himself. With you, I am convinced that
what we call 'unoccupied prayer' is a great act of faith
that affirms implicitly that God communicates lovingly with
us, at our centre, purifying and transforming us. What we
have to insist on over and over again is that this divine
communication, because divine, is not available to our
ordinary faculties and is, therefore, hidden. Hence the
sharpness of the test of faith.*

*Mark, I think we should leave the subject of consolations
as I feel that, by discussing it further we are giving it a
prominence it does not have. I think I have exhausted my
thought on it. What's more, I feel a lot of reflection and
analysis of it can make us self-conscious of our praying self,
whereas real prayer is 'off' self, uninterested in how it is
going, what is experienced and so forth. We go on praying
whatever the weather outside or in. It's as simple as that.
Of course, we all like lovely sunshine and find life easier
when there is plenty of it. But we in this country surely
know how to adapt ourselves to weather and not to bank
on a lovely day for this, that or the other. Surely we know
how to get on with life in spite of the weather? And, after
all, hasn't our 'weather' something to do with the formation
of our natural character, our enterprise and capacity to
soldier on doggedly? Inclement weather has advantages!
I feel we should aim at real indifference to weather*

conditions: getting on with living for God and others without much reflection on how we are feeling spiritually.

Once again I hold up Thérèse of Lisieux, truly the saint of ordinary folk like ourselves: 'Lord, you give me joy in all You do.' She was suffering atrociously in mind and body when she penned those words. This was faith, hope and love against all sensible feeling and this is what we try for. It's the joy Jesus wants to share with us, his joy which no one and nothing can ever deprive us of: 'Hitherto you have asked nothing in my name; ask and you will receive that your joy may be full' (John 16:24). To my mind, this has nothing to do with sensible joy though it may at times be accompanied by it. It is the joy, the solid content, the hope of absolute fulfilment based solely on Reality, the Reality of Abba as revealed by Jesus. And if we do want to look for real consolation, here it is. Sense may know little of it but the inmost heart knows and therefore can stand undaunted in every kind of spiritual weather and can humbly hope, relying on the 'promise of the Father' that, should great suffering come, it will still cry out in trust: 'Abba, my Father.' I think that Paul especially is the proclaimer of hope. 'We walk by faith and not by sight' (2 Corinthians 5:7) and yet have certain, unshakeable hope through the gift of the Spirit poured into our hearts. Romans 5:1–5 and 5:1–8 and 2 Corinthians 1–5 are most eloquent for me.

It is by faith and hope that we surrender ourselves to the Mystery of God who is Love absolute and this surrender is love. True love is ecstatic, outside self, a letting go of self and abdicating to Another. Herein lies personhood, a faint echo we surmise, of what we mean by 'person' when speaking of the Trinity. But, of course, we have Jesus our brother to show us and enable us to be truly human, truly person and just what that is, we cannot know in this life. We shall know when, for each of us, God is revealed, seen as God really is and in that vision, we become like Him and know our own reality which is reality only in Him. I believe that the transforming revelation begins in this life, in darkness and concealment. We must wait in hope for the revelation of our divine 'sonship'.

I'm not confident, dear Mark, that I have entered into your thought expressed in this letter before me, but I have tried to do so and offer you these reflections of mine as the best I can do.

With my love,

    Ruth

XXVII The road so far

Very dear Ruth,

Thank you for your wonderful letter. It was a splendid one: what you wrote about Hope was beautiful.

I like your shining a bright torch in the face of the fox consolation. Your words on Hope drew out the distinction which I sensed, but could not make. The fox stared back and then swung his face round over his shoulder and went loping off into the dark. Hope stayed on.

I remember once in the desert at night putting the headlights of the car on a wild cat. The Bedouin with me in the car were very excited and made me chase it. It got behind a tiny bush and watched us in that ridiculous way that cats have, thinking that they can't be seen. One of the Bedouin got out, went round in the dark, came up from behind and caught it up in a cloak. The wild cat was fearfully cross and stared at us with eyes of lemon contempt; huge front paws on short legs stretched wide on the cloak. I was struck by the mysterious silence of animals at such a moment. None of us knew what to say. Then with a laugh, we let it go and it ran (but at a 'let me get my dignity back' run, not a gallop) across the hard gravelly desert, into the night. And so much for consolations, then. Dismissed with the torch of good sense, or foolishly held for a moment of dumb encounter, off they go – into that unknown, that dark where, if we don't want to get really lost, we leave them be.

You say you are sure you're repeating yourself. I am sure I am myself here. But, you know, I don't think that matters either. It is another paradox that while each one's prayer is unique, yet it is the same. The Father, unlike what you beautifully describe as the weather in the soul, is the same. I think we have great difficulty in catching on to this – the unity of God in his limitless manifestations, all that you say about the sacrament of the Word and so on. I think the core points need repeating and repeating, in different phrases and colours; and we have to look and look, from all angles, before we recognise what we have seen, but not recognised, so many times before. Do you know, you said the same when I last saw you? I asked you what you said to your community about prayer, especially the younger ones who are newer to the very considerable regime of private prayer in your constitutions. You said in that low voice, 'Oh, always the same things.' Well, I don't think it's to be wondered at: the unity of what there is to be said and the difficulty we have in taking it in. Repetitious or not, here's what I had written to you before I got your letter:

> Very dear Ruth,
> When we started to write these letters, my own thinking was moved by a conviction that many people were frustrated in a desire to pray which somehow they were unable to convert into sustained prayer. Touched by the image of those who do pray and by the knowledge that the Church around the world is ceaselessly at prayer, they wanted actually to join in – for themselves and for others. But where and how to start? And my conviction that this impasse existed for many grew of course also out of myself. For this had been my own experience too.
>
> I remember so well my first visit to your monastery, ten years ago now, and going into the unlit church for Compline and realising suddenly that the members of the community were at their places in the choir, silent and in the dark. I knew that they were praying, but apart from that I could not say anything more about how they were

doing it. If I had tried to do the same, I should soon have been flinching and fidgeting at my own thoughts and distractions, quickly debating with myself where I had gone wrong because now, surely, I knew that I wasn't praying anymore.

I had read some books, looking for help. Some set out to teach how to pray. I was very interested in these because they appeared to offer to take the problem head on. But somehow they didn't. They offered techniques about how to sit quietly and about some people finding it helpful to create a 'praying corner' in the home. All this seemed like other people's Christmases – nice, of course, but ultimately happening at arm's length. At a deeper level, I had a horse sense that concentrating on technique was nothing more than concentrating on creating a state which I might enjoy and be able to say I had mastered. I could not accept that there wasn't something more than this to prayer.

Other books seemed to be about the life of the spirit in the widest sense. The writings of St Teresa and St John of the Cross and your own commentaries on their teaching describe the roads on which a soul must journey in its search for God and the difficulties which it must suffer before it may see that on every road Christ is in tireless search of the soul. These books certainly helped me. They gave cool water to the thirst which was in me. They taught me to laugh a bit more at my ineradicable selfishness and fascination with myself. They taught me a little more respect for the God who is and for his mysteries. I found I could pray more in snatches – at the traffic lights and on the pavement, waiting, and in gaps in conversation or work. What I didn't find was that I could kneel down, or sit down, and pray for more than a few minutes at a time. And I did try.

What was depressing was the notion which I found in several places in these books, that prayer was simple, 'The simplest thing out', 'If you want to pray, then pray!' I got frustrated with these observations. They seemed just plain contrary to real life – rather like the double take of a child when an exasperated grown up says, 'Apples don't grow on trees.' And I knew I wasn't alone. Friends knew of the same. Some had reached this point and had backed off. They might pray from time to time, go to Mass regularly, but they too were conscious that their prayer was very much what our busy end of century lives seemed to be able to afford: not much.

I worked out that we must be missing the point. Our idea of prayer must be off target. What was prayer, really? What was the bit which could last for a few moments and, if understood and allowed, could last for as long as . . . well, who knows? And we talked about this, you and I, and we agreed to look at it together in letters.

I have written all this down quickly because I caught myself this morning, thinking about a letter to you and spontaneously reflecting that the heart of prayer is simple, a heart and a simple one. Of course, it struck me that I was telling myself what once I had found so frustrating. I have been helped, as you so rightly pointed out a few letters ago. But it hasn't been just a matter of 'Hey, come off the grass . . . and pull your socks up!' My mind needed some assurance that what it should understand, it could understand. This might not be much, but the lack of it would be enough to snag the heart. Your Sister seemed to say she had found this was her case too.

In your letters you have explained the fundamentals. You say prayer is what God does in us. 'His faithful love endures for ever' (Psalms 106:1) and his expressing it in each unique human heart will be special to that heart. It may often be a mistake to offer advice to some one about how to pray. But each heart, as you said, does need help learning what prayer is. If another reads these letters of yours, as one or two have, and then reads them again, I think there is good hope she or he will be helped out of the impasse.

What has been valuable has been having the principles set out. How we as individuals react to these principles and develop our understanding of their implications in our own lives, must be an individual, and probably a long, matter of thought and prayer. The point is to make available some of the ideas which may remove the barriers, help us on to a further openness.

I think you have done that in a way which really does help. I am so grateful to you.

With much love,

   Mark

XXVIII Faith and accepting God's love

Dearest Mark,

Do you know, I feel like taking that wild cat by the scruff of its neck, shaking it until its teeth rattle and then throwing it off to slink away without dignity. But the wild cat for me is that ever-recurring, pestilential fidget about prayer, about how to do it and thinking one hasn't got it right. It's lack of faith, Mark.

The whole issue is one of faith and for us Christians that means choosing to believe in the God Jesus reveals to us and staking our life, everything, on this God. Here is the root of our problem. Prayer is no problem. It's lack of faith that is our problem. We don't really believe in the God of Jesus. Just to pick out one or two things from the gospel readings we have heard recently: ' . . . their angels in heaven always see the face of my Father who is in heaven' (Matthew 18:10), or, as some translate, 'are always in the presence of . . . ' We are those little ones and surely Jesus, who really knows, the one who speaks out of God, for God, is saying that our deepest essence is in God – inalienably. Think of those parables – of the lost sheep and the tenderness, the solicitude which will stop at nothing to rescue it; the father, yearning for his son's return and overwhelming him with love, rejoicing with a great joy. I could go on and on.

This is our God to whom each one of us is infinitely precious and whom He wants for himself – for He is our only happiness and fulfilment. And this God will move heaven and earth, will himself pay an appalling cost to bring us to himself. 'For it is not the will of my Father that one of these little ones be lost' (Matthew 18:14). This is the very heart of the gospel, of the Christian faith. Our labour is to believe. This, of course, calls for reading and reflection, as I said at the outset. But it's around these truthful images of Jesus' God that our thoughts should circulate, not around our own performance, our own little selves.

Get this right, really choose to believe through thick and thin and there can't be a problem, can there? You stand for many, I know, when you describe how you felt that evening at Compline. This idea that prayer is something difficult to get the hang of and no one seems ready to hand out the 'know-how' – there is no 'know-how'. If we believe in Jesus, we simply turn trustingly to our Father 'in Heaven'. Not 'up there', but in the most intimate, the most 'secret place' of ourselves, that is heaven (our angel, don't forget, is 'in Heaven'). We pray just as we are, in our pathetic reality. Grasp this and distractions don't matter, nor does the feeling of frustration and helplessness. Lay it all before this loving God; don't pretend to be other than you are. There is no need to perform or smarten ourselves up.

Once again, I reiterate, we believe or we don't. And we know we don't when we get worried because we can't get it right and no one will tell us. This comes from our need to affirm ourselves as God-orientated, prayerful, or whatever. We want to see ourselves praying. We must give that up, surrender in littleness, in rags and tatters and then there is no problem. If we don't believe, then there is nothing more I, or anyone else, can say, and certainly I would be the wrong person to approach since for me prayer is nothing more than affirming

God's love for me. *I stress the 'me' because unwittingly, we
can run away from a real encounter with God's absolute love
for me, by lots of concern for and praying for others. This
second concern must flow from the first and not* vice versa.
Our first 'duty' is to believe in God's love for me. *Isn't it easier
to cope with God's love in general? The lack of faith in God's
unique love for me, a failure to believe that the massive energy
of God's love is focused on me, that all He has done in giving
us Jesus is for me, as if I alone existed . . . isn't this the nub
when you think about it? Work on this, day and night, and you
have no problem.*

*If only we would grasp (and this means determine to believe
in) this most intimate relationship with God which is, in fact,
my very meaning, that is there, night and day, then prayer
would be like breathing. More, countless times a day we would
'remember' and address the loving Presence in some way or
other: a smile of love, a plea for help, a word of thanks . . . Of
course, setting time aside for prayer is important in any
Christian life, but it would not be difficult to claim that one
simply hasn't the time for an extended period of prayer – what
you mean by 'sustained prayer' – nor am I sure that is
everyone's calling at every time of life. But surely everyone
can afford five or ten minutes to give exclusively to God? No
one, however, can claim that they haven't the time to pray
throughout the day. All sorts of occasions present themselves:
in between interviews, going from one place to another,
from one task or another, waiting for someone, waking in the
night . . . If we believe, we shall want to do it, give it priority
and work at forming the habit. As faith develops, as well you
know, so does this living with God and surely the way we live
will accord with it. Our consciences will become sensitive and
we shall be quick to see when we have failed in love. And the
Answer is there at hand with open arms and the offer of
renewed strength. If only Christians would realise that prayer,*

*a life of deep intimacy with God is their very vocation; it is not
an 'extra', not a rather esoteric specialisation reserved for a
few, cranks or not.*

*You know, Mark, humility is a very, very important Christian
word not easily understood. To believe, to be just as we are
before God, to cast ourselves naked and powerless into God's
arms means the death of our natural pride, a very real, an ever
more radical death to the ego. To go back to the experience
you describe attending Compline – and I know you are
deliberately identifying with many – weren't you there really
wanting to be other than you are? Wanting to be in a different
spiritual 'place'? Well, that is just what has to be abandoned.
You must obstinately be who you are, as you are at the
moment, in that 'place' which seems so unfit, utterly unsuited
for a tête-à-tête with the All-Holy.*

*To say a few words about a more lengthened period of prayer.
Yes, I do think some sort of loosely held structure is needed,
but this must vary from person to person. Much has been
written on this and there are various 'schools' of prayer, in
that they teach a particular method. Whatever the method, it
is only a support for the mind, a sort of scaffolding. The
great thing in my experience is to remain relational, never
impersonal or abstract. Always encounter, listen to and
address the 'You'. If we are using a gospel story, be sure to
be face-to-face with Jesus, with him addressing us and us
responding to him, present in this moment, this now. My Lord
and my God – immediate to me. We are always in relationship
to God and cannot not be. God is always present in love and
loving action to me. Prayer, be it brief or extended, is simply a
loving remembrance and response to this Presence.*

*In relation to prayer, the sacraments are, of course, vital. To
neglect them is, to say the least, the height of folly. It's like*

*living in a house with pure, health-giving water laid on,
and insisting that we must go out and find our needful water,
digging for it all over the place, failing to recognise, or may be
refusing to recognise that the best of water is there at home,
completely available. We have only to turn on the kitchen tap
and hold out our vessels to be filled to the brim. Is it that
turning on the kitchen tap is just too ordinary, too easy?*

*I think our human pride comes in here, don't you? Our
sacraments – I think principally of the Eucharist and
Confession or Reconciliation – can outwardly be unattractive:
the form of celebration does not please us; the celebrant has
irritating mannerisms; the homily is not worth listening to; the
minister in the confessional gives the impression that he is
bored . . . it has to be admitted that, at times, there is that
which is justifiably judged offensive. But this is the reality of
Jesus' Church of sinners of which we ourselves are part, and it
is to this Church, within this Church, that Jesus gives us these
purifying, sanctifying sacraments to transform us into people
who can really love, really 'lay down' their lives for others,
people of whom it can be said that it is no longer they who
live, but Christ who lives in them.*

With my love,

Ruth

XXIX Prayer is faith

Very dear Ruth,

Poor old cat! I felt a bit sorry for him. I first read your letter
when I was feeling tired and my mind was worrying about
something else in the background. I found the letter a bit
tough. Now, I have read it again in a quite different temper,
can hear the characteristic tone of my friend's voice and I
smile. It is salutary, Ruth, the way you drive home these
important, hard points.

You remind me of Karl Rahner's way of speaking about the
'sacristy', his expression for religious activity which makes a
religious temperament (the lot of those in the first of your two
broad categories of those who pray) able to feel secure and
'better'. It doesn't have anything objectively to do with God,
but more with a subjective response to a psychic need. I take
the point of this metaphor to be that the sacristy is where the
vestments are kept and other bits and pieces. It's not where the
altar is. The sacristy can be where we 'dress up' as Christians
and tell ourselves we are the better for it. In the language of
this last letter of yours it's where we hide the real 'me' in the
comforting, familiar robes of 'religion'. Yes, dithering about
prayer, whether hovering in the sacristy or just not getting on
with it, must be about lack of faith. I take your comments to be
emphatically underlining the danger that we may really be
most protecting, enclosing our inmost selves when we actually
think we are most 'opening' ourselves to God.

You're right, really, to keep putting your finger back on faith. It is where we started out. Sure, faith is the problem. Sure, the lack of faith is the nub. But I think it's very important for those who don't have easy access to advice, carefully to distinguish between personal weakness in approaching faith – what you mean by the ego, and weak faith itself which is, I think, a different matter. Personally, I don't mind weak faith too much. What can I do? I have to live with it. I know it strengthens in some way, but it's never the faith my ego would like to have. It's the faith I know I've got. It's real to me even in its weakness and I got to know it better by not fretting whether there was a lot I could do about it. Watching paint dry came to mind. It's perfectly obvious that fretting must be bad for faith, but that doesn't mean it's easy to avoid. I hung on to Jesus' teaching us 'always to pray and not to lose heart' (Luke 18:1) which I understood also to mean that we should have good heart where we are. I am glad that you seemed to agree with this in your letter.

Here at the end, in answer to my very first question, 'What is prayer?', all I can say today is, 'Prayer is faith; faith is prayer.' What we do about that conclusion is the expression of how much we accept it. I think that would sound unhelpfully abstract but for your practical sense. What a help you've been. I'm so grateful to you for putting up with all the trouble I've put you to.

With much love,

Mark

XXX Prayer and love

Very dear Ruth,

It was very good to see you last week – you gave me a very
happy time. There was so much to talk about we only had time
to touch on our last exchange of letters. So you said, 'Write
down what you've just said . . . '

I said that in your last letter to me I thought you had widened
your comments to a more general idea of prayer which
included 'All sorts of occasions . . . in between interviews'
and so on. The point you were making about faith was the
important thing to say, but it didn't immediately take care
of the imperative for private prayer (which you usually
underline). So we found the question between us still open:
'Why don't people pray?' It is odd, isn't it, that people don't
pray more. What, really, do you think are the barriers?

In the 'penny' catechism, the answer to the second question,
'Why did God make you?', is 'To know Him, love Him and
serve Him in this world and to be happy with Him for ever in
the next.' We can take it that the life to which we are called is,
in summary, a life of prayer. I think that's what you were
saying in emphasising prayer as the natural expression of a real
faith. So prayer encompasses these three elements: knowing,
loving, and serving. And within easy limits don't we do our
bit? We do try to get to know Him – we read, pay attention in
church and reflect, and we do try to serve Him – crucially in

service of others. We know how imperfect and impure our motives really are in these efforts, but all around efforts are being made. As the beneficiaries of others' efforts we really can say, 'Ave, Christe!' We can be encouraged.

I wonder if we don't have a much greater problem with loving God. Aren't we caught between the psychological horror of a helpless negative ('I do not love God') and the unfathomable phenomenon of those souls which declare their passionate, zealous, 'in-love' love of God? Doesn't private prayer which offers the mind so little and appears empty of our human ideas of service, pose this stark question, 'How do I love You?' We ask the question of God; He asks it of us. And so little have we plumbed the allegories of human emotional and physical love that perhaps we find it hard to answer the question – ours and His.

I think that there can be a block here in private prayer on two levels. First, when we ask ourselves, 'How do I love You?', isn't the sincere reply just a sense of unworthiness, a deep awareness of our sinfulness? We have nothing effective to say. It's all so different from our own experience of giving love, whether in wooing a loved one, being kind and warm to a small child, or caring for someone in distress. Secondly, and this can be daunting against the background of the devotional vocabulary of the saints, the question frames itself, 'How can I love You?' We are on a dimension which, as you said, is 'not available to our ordinary consciousness'. The self recalls the psalmist's cry, 'Lord, hide not your face'(Psalms 102:2). Humanly, love on the dimension of faith is a mystery and I think private prayer can falter on it. Isn't it safer, then, and wiser to allow divine love to be itself on its own plane? We cannot but receive. We cannot give to God in the abstract. We can only give Him what is His to give us first.

I mentioned in an earlier letter the impact on me of Jesus' statement to the rich young man that 'only God is good' (Mark 10:18). When I put this together with the affirmation that 'prayer is what God does in us' and join them with this question about love, the next line writes itself: 'Love too is what God does in us.' I took this to the great discourse of Jesus after the Last Supper in St John and, after the resurrection, his exchange with Peter on the shore of Lake Tiberias. Throughout, Jesus defines our love as our choice to do as he asks – in keeping his commandments (John 14:15), especially in loving one another (John 14:21), and for Peter in feeding his sheep (John 21:17). Jesus tells the disciples, 'Remain in my love' (John 15:10). How rightly you emphasised in your last letter the 'me' in saying that 'prayer is nothing more than affirming God's love for me'. Jesus speaks often of the love he has from the Father, of the love he has for us, of the love we are to have for one another, if we remain in his love. This love is mysterious, but it initiates and propagates – 'He loved us first' (I John 4:19). It derives from the Father and we know it through the Son. Don't we make our reply to this gift of love, this being in His love, by turning to prayer?

These gifts of faith, hope and love are absolute and absolutely given. Prayer, the encounter in secret with the Absolute, is mediated for us by the Spirit in Jesus in whom alone we know the human meaning of these infinite gifts to us.

With much love,

    Mark

XXXI A living love – a living prayer

Dearest Mark,

I enjoyed our talks just as much as you did. It's no good going to the parlour without a thinking cap when you are on the other side. And now I have your letter to wrestle with.

'To know, love and serve God' : such is the meaning of our life, a meaning revealed by faith. That is the operative word: faith that is a gift, an empowerment that demands constant use. To allow our lives to be governed by faith is to live a life of prayer and, one day perhaps, to be a living prayer. Prayer is self-surrender in faith: faith is self-surrender, abandoning our own little ship of which we have the control, knowing its ropes, as we say, and crossing over into the boat of Jesus which we cannot control. The Holy Spirit alone knows the ins and outs of this craft. Faith/prayer is living out the love-relationship between ourselves and God.

Mark, I am certain that we must not be fascinated by what the old hagiographers delighted in recounting of the saints, such as 'declarations of their passionate, zealous, being "in-love" with God'. Of themselves these things mean very little. Temperament, psycho-physical factors, especially when, as in most cases, the subject is a woman, prevailing cultural notions of holiness and the expectancy they evoke – these and other purely natural things play a huge part in religious experiences. I make so bold as to say that I think even the great saints were guilty of some self-indulgence here. Emotion can be whipped up and feeds on itself. Just as we can augment feelings of misery and self-pity simply by dwelling on them and rehearsing their cause, so we can foment the 'torment' of love and, in the spiritual life, this can seem authenticating, proof to ourselves and others that we do indeed love God, and Oh, how passionately we long for some proof, some assurance coming from our inner experience that we do love God!

There is no doubt that in some cases the intensity of emotion matched the reality of love, but the reality of love is an ever-growing generosity and selflessness. You can have the latter without the former and vice versa. It remains an objective truth that we simply cannot assume that our state of feeling whatever it be, tells us the truth of how things really are between ourselves and God – or even other people. Commonsense knows this but we fail to apply it to the spiritual life. I never want to run down emotion in the spiritual life. Far from it. It can be enormously helpful and one could imagine that, in an ideal world, our emotional state would accord with reality – we don't know. If spiritual emotion leads us, as it should, to greater generosity, then it is a blessing. But we may not rely on it, nor seek it, nor wring our hands in despair and give up when it is absent.

Ultimately, faith in God's love for each one of us, assures us that, if consolations of whatever kind would help us to love more, they will come. If they don't come, then we can be quite sure that we do not need them and can love God more without them. It is love of God we are after, isn't it? Not self-satisfaction.

Like you, Mark, I shrink from the assertion that I love God. The statement has a ring of claim, of achievement, and of

*lifting myself up a little on my own wings. I can honestly say
that I want to love God and that I try to do so, and objectively
I know this is love, but what a puny love! The conviction of
Thérèse of Lisieux, however, that confidence, boundless
confidence alone must lead us to love, is mine also. It seems it
is what the gospel says and you point out instances in the
gospel of John. Jesus directs us to loving our neighbour,
keeping his commandment of love for others 'as I have loved
you' – that is to the point of total self-emptying. Such a love,
his love, can only be given. Our part is to believe that it will be
given, and in this confidence doing our utmost to love.*

*To take up the incident of the rich young man in Mark's gospel,
I am deeply impressed by its conclusion – 'Who then can be
saved?', ask the bewildered disciples; and Jesus replies in
effect, 'No one.' It is impossible for human beings to be
saved. God must do it, can and will. Jesus alone knows the full
content of being saved, something that exceeds all our thinking
and imagining and is quite beyond our powers. It is, as often
expressed, a sharing in the life of God. Have you noticed the
juxtaposition of this story with that of the little children being
brought to Jesus and these same important men trying to
prevent this? Jesus rebukes them, emphasising once again the
real truth of the matter: vis-à-vis God we are as helpless,
dependent as very small children – but cherished children. Oh,
how hard it is to take this seriously! How hard it is for us who
have riches, who rely in any way on ourselves, who want to
claim our virtue, our good works, who at bottom, seek to save
ourselves, to enter the kingdom of God! Here lies our spiritual
blindness. It is a great thing even to glimpse this truth and
so turn in the right direction. Over and over again, if we
have an inkling of it, we catch ourselves out in spiritual
self-importance, secretly preening ourselves at our success and
goodness, working as if we were the artisans of our destiny,
despairing at our failures. I steady myself with the simple*

*reflection, 'After all, I am only a tiny child in God's eyes.' That
puts things in perspective!*

*To deny that we have any love for God would be to deny our
redemption. It would deny too, the wonderful words of Paul
that 'The love of God has been poured into our hearts by the
Holy Spirit who has been given to us' (Romans 5:5). He is
saying that God enables us to love as He enables us to believe.
(Can there be a separation between faith and love? I can't see
how.) In the gift of the Holy Spirit we are given God's own love
to love Him with. That is our faith. But our cry of distress and
anxiety spring from keen awareness of our selfishness and lack
of generosity, of the impurity of our motives and the overall
shoddiness of our lives, and we are asking, 'Am I really
responding to this love, allowing it to permeate my life?' There
seems little proof. You yourself indicate the only course there
is: to go on trying, with the light we have, to do God's will, to
read, reflect, pray and beg for light, to be shown what God
asks and where we are not giving . . . and then boundless
confidence, stubborn confidence in the goodness, the
unconditional love of God.*

*God is at work in me at every moment, purifying me of
selfishness, transforming me and drawing me into a union with
himself that will be revealed only when I die. Love waits on
Love's will and Love's time and makes no demands. I think it is
'unoccupied' prayer that most expresses this blind trust, the
conviction that God must do it and God will.*

*So, dear Mark, to borrow Thérèse's words, let us keep far
away from all that glitters, love our poverty, be content not to
have the joy of seeing how beautiful and dear we are in God's
eyes. Yes, beautiful, because when we cling to Him in our daily
activity, liturgical worship and solitary prayer, He is able to
love us and make us beautiful. So quietly, we fold our fretting,*

anxious wings and, like the gull, rest on the ocean of God's love which bears us, mysteriously, into Its depths, the haven we desire.

With my love,

    Ruth